EGYPTIAN ART STUDIES

BY

SIR GASTON MASPERO

Hon. K.C.M.G., Hon. D.C.L., and Fellow of Queen's College, Oxford

Member of the Institute of France, Professor at the Collège de France, Director-General of the Service des Antiquités, Cairo

TRANSLATED BY ELIZABETH LEE

WITH 107 ILLUSTRATIONS

ISBN: 978-1-63923-548-3

All Rights reserved. No part of this book maybe reproduced without written permission from the publishers, except by a reviewer who may quote brief passages in a review to be printed in a newspaper or magazine.

Printed: February 2023

Published and Distributed By:
Lushena Books
607 Country Club Drive, Unit E
Bensenville, IL 60106
www.lushenabks.com

ISBN: 978-1-63923-693-0

PREFATORY NOTE

THE following essays were written during a period of more than thirty years, and published at intervals of varying lengths. The oldest of them appeared in *Les Monuments de l'Art Antique* of my friend Olivier Rayet, and the others in *La Nature* at the request of Gaston Tissandier, in the *Gazette des Beaux-Arts*, in the *Monuments Piot*, and chiefly in the *Revue de l'Art Ancien et Moderne*, where my friend Jules Comte gave them hospitality. As most of these periodicals do not circulate in purely scientific circles, the essays are almost unknown to experts, and will for the greater part be new to them. Indeed, they were not intended for them. In writing them, I desired to familiarize the general public, who were scarcely aware of their existence, with some of the fine pieces of Egyptian sculpture and goldsmiths' work, and to point out how to approach them in order to appreciate their worth. Some, after various vicissitudes, had found a home in the Museums of Paris or of Cairo, and I wrote the notices in my study, deducing at leisure the reasons for my criticisms. Others I caught as they emerged from the ground, the very day of or the day after their discovery, and I described them on the spot, as it were, under the influence of my first encounter with them: they themselves dictated to me what I said of them.

Some persons will perhaps be surprised to find the same ideas developed at length in several parts of the book. If

Prefatory Note

they will carry their thoughts back to the date at which I wrote, they will recognize the necessity of such repetitions. Egyptologists, absorbed in the task of deciphering, had eyes for scarcely anything except the historical or religious literary texts; and so amateurs or inquirers, finding nothing in the works of experts to help them to any sound interpretation of the characteristic manifestations of Egyptian art, were reduced to register them without always understanding them, for lack of knowledge of the concepts that had imposed their forms on them. It is now admitted that such objects of art are above all utilitarian, and that they were originally commissioned with the fixed purpose of assuring the well-being of human survival in an existence beyond the grave. Thirty years ago, few were aware of this, and to convince the rest, it was necessary to insist continually on the proofs and to multiply examples. I might of course have suppressed a portion of them here, but had I done so, should I not have been reproached, and quite rightly, with misrepresenting and almost falsifying a passage in the history of the Egyptian arts? The ideas which govern our present conception did not at once reach the point where they now are. They came into being one after the other, and spread themselves by successive waves of unequal intensity, welcomed with favour by some, rejected by others. I had to begin over again a dozen times and in a dozen different ways before I obtained their almost universal acceptation. I was at first laughed at when I put forward the opinion that there was not one unique art in Egypt, identical from one extremity of the valley to the other except for almost imperceptible nuances of execution, but that there were at least half a dozen local schools, each with its own traditions and its own principles, often divided into several studios, the technique of which I

Prefatory Note

tried to determine. In the end the incredulous rallied to my side, and it would have been bad grace on my part to leave out of the articles which helped to convert them, at least I hope so, the repetitions which led to their being convinced.

Besides, I am sure that they will render my readers of to-day the same service that they rendered formerly to my colleagues in Egyptology. When they have thoroughly entered into the spirit of the Egyptian ideas concerning existence in this world and the next, they will understand what Egyptian art is, and why it is above everything realistic. The question for Egyptian art was not to create a type of independent beauty in the person of the individuals who furnish the principal elements of it, but to express truthfully the features which constituted that person and which must be preserved identical as long as anything of him persisted among the living and the dead. But why should I epitomize here in a necessarily incomplete way ideas which are amply set forth in the book itself? I shall do better in using the small space left me in thanking the publishers who have kindly authorized me to reproduce the illustrations which accompanied my articles, Jules Comte, the directors of *La Nature*, and my old friends of the firm of Hachette. They have thus collaborated in this book, and it will owe a large part of its success to their kindness.

CONTENTS

	PAGE
PREFATORY NOTE	5

I
EGYPTIAN STATUARY AND ITS SCHOOLS 17

II
SOME PORTRAITS OF MYCERINUS 36

III
A SCRIBE'S HEAD OF THE IVTH OR VTH DYNASTY . . . 49

IV
SKHEMKA, HIS WIFE AND SON : A GROUP FOUND AT MEMPHIS . 55

V
THE CROUCHING SCRIBE : VTH DYNASTY 60

VI
THE NEW SCRIBE OF THE GIZEH MUSEUM 66

VII
THE KNEELING SCRIBE : VTH DYNASTY 74

VIII
PEHOURNOWRI : STATUETTE IN PAINTED LIMESTONE FOUND AT MEMPHIS 79

Contents

IX	PAGE
THE DWARF KHNOUMHOTPOU : VTH OR VITH DYNASTY	85
X	
THE "FAVISSA" OF KARNAK, AND THE THEBAN SCHOOL OF SCULPTURE	90
XI	
THE COW OF DEÎR-EL-BAHARÎ	106
XII	
THE STATUETTE OF AMENÔPHIS IV	120
XIII	
FOUR CANOPIC HEADS FOUND IN THE VALLEY OF THE KINGS AT THEBES	126
XIV	
A HEAD OF THE PHARAOH HARMHABI	135
XV	
THE COLOSSUS OF RAMSES II AT BEDRECHEÎN	140
XVI	
EGYPTIAN JEWELLERY IN THE LOUVRE	145
XVII	
THE TREASURE OF ZAGAZIG	154
XVIII	
THREE STATUETTES IN WOOD	172

Contents

XIX
A Fragment of a Theban Statuette	PAGE 178

XX
A The Lady Touî of the Louvre and Egyptian Industrial Sculpture in Wood 183

XXI
Some Perfume Ladles of the XVIIIth Dynasty . . 190

XXII
Some Green Basalt Statuettes of the Saïte Period . 195

XXIII
A Find of Saïte Jewels at Saqqarah 201

XXIV
A Bronze Egyptian Cat belonging to M. Barrère . . 208

XXV
A Find of Cats in Egypt 214

Index 217

ILLUSTRATIONS

	FACING PAGE
THE MYCERINUS OF MÎT-RAHINEH	38
MYCERINUS (REISNER HEAD)	38
ALABASTER STATUE OF MYCERINUS	40
MYCERINUS, HATHOR, AND THE NOME OXYRRHINCHUS	42
MYCERINUS, HATHOR, AND THE NOME CYNOPOLITE	42
MYCERINUS AND HIS WIFE	44
MYCERINUS, HATHOR, AND THE NOME OF THE SISTRUM	46
MYCERINUS AND HIS WIFE (DETAIL)	46
MYCERINUS AND HIS WIFE (DETAIL)	48
SCRIBE'S HEAD	50
SKHEMKA WITH HIS WIFE AND SON	56
CROUCHING SCRIBE	60
THE NEW SCRIBE OF THE GIZEH MUSEUM	66
STATUE OF RÂNOFIR	72
KNEELING SCRIBE	74
PEHOURNOWRI	80
THE DWARF KHNOUMHOTPOU	86
THE WORKS AT KARNAK IN JANUARY, 1906	92
MONTOUHOTPOU V	94
HEAD OF A COLOSSUS OF SANOUOSRÎT	94
SANOUOSRÎT AND THE GOD PHTAH	94
BUST OF THOUTMÔSIS III	96
ISIS, MOTHER OF THOUTMÔSIS III	96

Illustrations

	FACING PAGE
SANMAOUT AND THE PRINCESS NAFÊROURÎYA	98
STATUETTE IN PETRIFIED WOOD	100
THEBAN KHONSOU	100
STATUE OF TOUTÂNOUKHAMANOU	100
THE SO-CALLED TAIA	100
RAMSES II	100
RAMSES IV LEADING A LIBYAN CAPTIVE	100
THE PRIEST WITH THE MONKEY	102
OSORKON II OFFERING A BOAT TO THE GOD AMON	104
QUEEN ANKHNASNOFIRIABRÊ	104
MANTIMEHÊ	104
NSIPHTAH, SON OF MANTIMEHÊ	104
HEAD (SAÏTE PERIOD)	104
THE COW OF DEÎR-EL-BAHARÎ IN HER CHAPEL	104
AMENÔTHES II AND THE COW HATHOR	106
AMENÔTHES II AND THE COW HATHOR	106
THE COW HATHOR	108
AN UNKNOWN FIGURE AND THE COW HATHOR	112
PETESOMTOUS AND THE COW HATHOR	114
PSAMMETICHUS AND THE COW HATHOR	116
PSAMMETICHUS AND THE COW HATHOR	118
AMENÔPHIS IV	120
KING KHOUNIATONOU	126
KING KHOUNIATONOU	126
KING KHOUNIATONOU	128
KING KHOUNIATONOU	130
KING KHOUNIATONOU	130
QUEEN TÎYI (FULL FACE)	130

Illustrations

	FACING PAGE
QUEEN TÎYI (PROFILE)	130
PRINCESS OF THE FAMILY OF TÎYI (PROFILE)	132
PRINCESS OF THE FAMILY OF TÎYI (FULL FACE)	132
KING KHOUNIATONOU	132
KING KHOUNIATONOU	134
HEAD OF THE PHARAOH HARMHABI	136
THE HALF-BURIED COLOSSUS OF RAMSES II	140
THE COLOSSUS OF RAMSES II EMERGING FROM THE EARTH	140
EGYPTIAN JEWELLERY OF THE XIXTH DYNASTY	146
GOLD PECTORAL INLAID WITH ENAMEL	146
PECTORAL OF RAMSES II	148
PECTORAL IN SHAPE OF A HAWK WITH A RAM'S HEAD	148
SILVER BRACELETS AND EARRINGS	156
GOLD EARRING FROM THE TREASURE OF ZAGAZIG	156
ONE OF RAMSES II'S BRACELETS (OPEN)	158
ONE OF RAMSES II'S BRACELETS (CLOSED)	158
GOLD CUP OF QUEEN TAOUASRÎT	160
SMALLER OF THE TWO GOLD VASES (FRONT VIEW)	160
SMALLER OF THE TWO GOLD VASES (BACK VIEW)	162
MASS OF SILVER VASES SOLDERED TOGETHER BY OXIDE	162
LARGER OF THE TWO GOLD VASES (FRONT VIEW)	164
LARGER OF THE TWO GOLD VASES (BACK VIEW)	164
THE VASE WITH THE KID	164
ONE OF THE SILVER PATERÆ OF ZAGAZIG (SIDE VIEW)	166
SILVER STRAINER	166
THE BOTTOM OF ONE OF THE ZAGAZIG SILVER PATERAE	168
STATUETTES IN WOOD	172
THE MOND STATUETTE (FRONT VIEW)	178

Illustrations

	FACING PAGE
THE MOND STATUETTE (PROFILE)	180
THE LADY TOUÎ, STATUETTE IN WOOD	184
STATUETTE IN WOOD	186
STATUETTE IN WOOD	186
PERFUME LADLE	190
PERFUME LADLE	190
PERFUME LADLE	192
PERFUME LADLE	192
PERFUME LADLE	194
GREEN BASALT STATUETTES OF THE SAÏTE PERIOD	196
NECKLACE AMULET	202
VULTURE AMULET	202
GOLD PALM-TREE	202
BOAT OF SOKARIS	202
RAM'S HEAD	202
GOLD HAWK	202
HAWK WITH HUMAN HEAD	202
HAWK WITH RAM'S HEAD	202
VULTURE	202
ISIS WITH THE CHILD	202
CROUCHING NEÎTH	202
MONKEYS WORSHIPPING THE EMBLEM OF OSIRIS	204
VULTURE WITH EXTENDED WINGS	204
HAWK WITH EXTENDED WINGS	204
THE SOUL (FRONT VIEW)	204
THE SOUL (BACK VIEW)	204
BRONZE CAT OF THE SAÏTE PERIOD	208
BRONZE CAT	214

EGYPTIAN ART

I

EGYPTIAN STATUARY AND ITS SCHOOLS*

I OPENED F. W. von Bissing's work † with a certain feeling of melancholy, for it was a thing that I had hoped to do myself. Ebers had suggested to Bruckmann, the publisher, that he should entrust the task to me, and I was on the point of arranging with him when the preparations for an Orientalist Congress to meet at Paris in 1897 deprived me of the leisure left me by my lectures and the printing of my "History," and I was forced to give up the project. Herr von Bissing, who was less occupied then than I was, consented to hazard the adventure, and no one could have been better equipped than he was to carry it through. The seeking of materials, the execution of typographical *clichés*, the composition of the text and its careful setting forth exacted eight years of travelling and continuous labour. Bissing issued the first part at the end of 1905, and five other parts have quickly followed, forming almost the half of the work, seventy-two plates folio, and the portions of the explanatory text belonging to the plates.

* From the *Journal des Savants*, 1908, pp. 1-17.
† F. W. von Bissing, "Denkmäler Ægyptischer Skulptur." Text, 4to; portfolio of plates, fol.; Bruckmann, Munich, 1906-8.

Studies in Egyptian Art

I

The title is not, at least as yet, exactly accurate. Egyptian sculpture includes, in fact, besides statues and groups in alto-relievo, bas-reliefs often of very large dimensions which adorn the tombs or the walls of temples. Now Bissing has only admitted statues and groups to the honours of publication: the few specimens of the bas-reliefs that he gives are not taken from the ruins themselves, but have been selected from pieces in the museums, stelæ, or fragments of ruined buildings. It is then the monuments of Egyptian statuary that he presents to us rather than those of Egyptian sculpture as a whole.

Having made that statement and thus defined the extent of the field of action, it must be frankly admitted that he has always made a happy selection of pieces to be reproduced. Doubtless we may regret the absence of some famous pieces, such as the Crouching Scribe of the Louvre or the Cow of Deir el-Bahari. The fault is not his, and perhaps he will succeed in overcoming the obstacles which forced him to deprive us of them. The omissions, at any rate, are not numerous. When the list printed on the covers of the first part is exhausted, amateurs and experts will have at their disposal nearly everything required to follow the evolution of Egyptian statuary from its earliest beginnings to the advent of Christianity. The schools of the Greek and Roman epochs, unjustly contemned by archæologists who have written on these subjects, are not wanting, and for the first time the ordinary reader can decide for himself if all the artists of the decadence equally deserve contempt or oblivion. Bissing has attempted a complete picture, not a sketch restricted to the principal events in art between the IVth

Egyptian Statuary

Dynasty and the XXXth. No serious attempt of the kind had before been made, and on many points he had to open out the roads he traversed. For the moment he has stopped at the beginning of the Saïte period; thus we have as yet no means of judging if the plan he has imposed on himself is carried out to the end with a rigour and firmness everywhere equal: but a rapid examination of the parts that have appeared will show that it has been executed with fullness and fidelity.

Four plates are devoted to Archaic Egypt: the two first are facsimiles of the bas-reliefs that decorate the stele of the Horus Qa-âou, and the so-called *palette* of the king we designate Nâr-mer, since we have not deciphered his name. It is in truth very little, but the excavations have rendered such poor accounts of those distant ages that it is almost all that could be given of them; it might, however, have been worth while to add the statuettes of the Pharaoh Khâsakhmouî. Notwithstanding the omission, the objects that appear give a sufficient idea of the degree of skill attained by the sculptors of those days. The stele of Qa-âou does not, of course, equal that of the *King-Serpent* * which is in the Louvre; it is, however, of a fairly good style, and the hawk of Horus is nearer to the real animal than those of the protocol were later. Similarly the scenes engraved on the *palette* of Nâr-mer testify to an indisputable virtuosity in the manner of attacking the stone. The drawing of the persons is less schematic and their bearing freer than in the compositions of classical art, but it is evident that the craftsman had as yet no very clear idea of the way in which to compose a picture and

* It may also be asked if the stele of the King-Serpent is an original or a restoration of the time of Setouî I.

Studies in Egyptian Art

group its elements. Let us confess, nevertheless, that the bas-reliefs are far superior to the statues yet known. We possess about half a dozen of them scattered over the world. Bissing studied one to the exclusion of the others, the one in the Naples Museum, and it may be thought to be sufficient if only æsthetic impressions are desired, for nothing could be rougher or more awkward. The head and face might perhaps pass, but the rest is ill-proportioned, the neck is too short, the shoulders and chest are massive, the legs lack slenderness under a heavy petticoat, the feet and hands are enormous. The defects cannot be ascribed to the hardness of the material, for the Scribe of the Cairo Museum, which is in limestone, displays them as flagrantly as the good people in granite at Naples, Munich, or Leyden. I must not therefore conclude, however, that they are constant faults with the Thinites: the statuettes of Khâsakhmouî are of a less heavy workmanship and more nearly approach that of later studios. That the ruins have rendered only a few that possess worth does not prove that there may not have been excellent ones: we must have patience and wait till some happy chance belies the mediocrity.

The Memphian Empire has furnished thirteen plates, and I doubt if they are enough. The number of masterpieces, and especially of pieces which, without possessing claims to perfection, offer interest on some count, is so large that Bissing could easily have found, in the Cairo Museum alone, material enough to double the number. Very probably it was due to the publisher and a question of economy: but all the same I regret the absence of half a dozen statues that would have made a good appearance by the side of the Scribe of the Berlin Museum. The chief species of the period are at least represented

Egyptian Statuary

by very good examples: statues of the Pharaoh seated, receiving homage, are represented by two of the Chephrên of the Cairo Museum; of the Pharaoh standing, by the Pioupi in bronze; those of private individuals standing and isolated, or in groups, by the Cheikh el-Beled of the Gizeh Museum, by the Sapoui and the Nasi of the Louvre, or by the pair at Munich; those of individuals seated by the Scribe of Berlin and by one of the Readers of Cairo. One of the Cairo statues, of mediocre workmanship, is, however, curious, because it shows us a priest completely nude, by no means usual, and circumcized, a fact still less usual. Three fragments preserved at Munich, portions of three stelæ, a complete stele from the Cairo Museum, an episode borrowed from the tomb of Apoui, of which Cairo possesses almost an entire wall, provide specimens of bas-reliefs for the student to study, without, however, permitting him to suspect the variety of motives and abundance of detail usually met with in the necropolises of Saqqarah or of Gizeh. Reduced to these elements, Bissing's book will make the impression on its readers of a noble art exalted by inspiration, minute and skilful in the material execution, but monotonous, and confined in a rather narrow circle of concepts and forms of expression. It is only fair to add that the book is not finished and that, thanks to the system employed of double and triple plates, it is quite easy to insert new documents among those of the parts that have already appeared. Some of the lacunæ will assuredly be filled up, and the additions will place us in a better position to judge the worth of the ancient Memphian school.

The notices of the first Theban Empire are more numerous, and they render it possible to study the

Studies in Egyptian Art

history of statuary during the long interval that separates the Heracleopolitan period from the domination of the Shepherd Kings. For the XIth Dynasty, besides the wonderful statue of Montouhotpou III, there are bas-reliefs or paintings found at Gebelein in the ruins of a temple of Montouhotpou 1. Afterwards, we have, in the XIIth Dynasty itself, the seated statues of Sanouosrît I, of Nofrît and of Amenemhaît III, the sphinx of Amenemhaît III that Mariette declared to be the portrait of a Hyksôs king, an admirable king's head preserved in the Vienna Museum, and pieces of lesser interest, among which a curious bas-relief of Sanouosrît I dancing before the god Minou at Coptos should be mentioned. For the XIIIth and following Dynasties, I only see as yet the Sovkhotpou of the Louvre, the barbarous head of Mit-Fares, and the Sovkemsaouf of Vienna, but we must wait for the next parts before deciding to what point Bissing has made use of the rich store of documents available for that period. The second Theban Empire, so rich in souvenirs of all kinds, offered an embarrassing choice: the Cairo Museum alone possesses material enough for two or three volumes, especially since the fortunate excavations conducted by Legrain at the *favissa* of Karnak. The subjects in favour of which Bissing decided have their special importance: they are each the actual head of a pillar, the type of a series that he could, in many cases, have reproduced almost entire, so well has chance served us in the course of these last years. The statues of Amenôthes, of Thoutmôsis, of the Ramses, of the Harmais are celebrated, and it is unnecessary to enumerate them one after the other: the reader will see them again with pleasure as he goes along, and will admire the marvellous skill with which the photographer has reproduced

Egyptian Statuary

them, and the printer has responded to the photographer's skill. The pictures of the volume are often perfect, and plates like those of the head of one of the sphinxes of Amenemhaît III are so successful that in looking at them we have almost the sensation of the original. In a few, however, the printing is too heavy and the thickness of the ink has distorted and coarsened the modelling. As a general rule the larger number of the defects I have noted are due to this tiresome question of inks. I know too well from my own experience the difficulties caused by the obstinacy of the workmen on that point, so I am able to make excuses for both Bruckmann and Bissing.

II

So much for the illustrations: the portion of the text as yet published greatly increases their interest, and assures the work permanent value. It contains information as to the origin of the object, its migrations, its actual home to-day, its state of preservation and, at need, the restorations it has undergone: descriptions showing careful research, and extended bibliographies complete the suggestions made by the picture, and inform us of previous criticisms. The shortest of the notices fills two compact quarto columns, and are reinforced by numerous footnotes; many of them are veritable essays in which the subject is examined on every side and as exhaustively as is possible. Vignettes are inserted which exhibit the object in a different light from that of the plate, or show the reader some of the analogous motives referred to in the discussion.

Repetition of similar types has sometimes prevented Bissing from developing his views as a whole, and we

Studies in Egyptian Art

are compelled to look under several rubrics before learning his full opinion. This is a serious drawback unless it is remedied in the introduction: we shall perhaps find all the observations brought together there into one system, with justificatory references to each of the notices in particular.

Bissing's criticisms are always well justified: they testify to a mature taste or a sure tact, and there are very few with which experts would not willingly agree. Here and there, however, I must make some reservations, for example, with regard to the Chephrên of Gizeh. After discussing at length Borchardt's reasons for attributing it to a Saïte school, and refuting them, Bissing declares that it is perhaps a late copy of a work contemporary with the Pharaoh. I recently had occasion to study it closely in order to determine the position in the Museum best suited to it, and to decide the height of the plinth on which it should be placed. I went over Borchardt's arguments and Bissing's hypotheses one after the other and came to the conclusion that the date assigned by Mariette at the moment of its discovery is the only admissible one. The archæological details belong to the Memphian age, and the peculiarities of style which Bissing points out, and which actually exist, are not sufficiently strongly marked to justify its attribution to a later epoch. I only see in them the divergences which, in every age, mark works coming from different and perhaps rival studios. The artists who cut the *doubles* in diorite destined for the pyramid of the Pharaoh, did not certainly have the same masters as those to whom we owe the Chephrên in alabaster and the royal statuettes of Mitrahineh: the difference of origin sufficiently explains why they do not resemble each other. I fear that in criticizing

Egyptian Statuary

certain sculptures Borchardt and others were governed in spite of themselves by the ideas that long prevailed on the uniformity and monotony of Egyptian art. It seemed to them that at one and the same period the composition and inspiration must always remain identical, and wherever they did not harmonize, the fact was attributed solely to an interval in time. But we must accustom ourselves to think that things did not go differently with the Egyptians than with the moderns. In a city like Memphis there was more than one studio, and they all possessed their traditions, their affectations, their style, which distinguished them from each other, and which are found in their work like a trade-mark. Some errors of classification will be avoided in the future if we can be persuaded to recognize that many of the peculiarities that we begin to note on statues and bas-reliefs may be the mannerisms of the school to which they belong, and are not always indications of relative age.

The care that Bissing has taken to render what is due to each of the experts who discovered a piece or spoke of it, deserves the more praise since many Egyptologists of the present generation have adopted the attitude of ignoring what has been said or written before them. They seem to insinuate to their readers that archæology, religion, grammar, history, nothing indeed that they touch on, has ever been studied before, and that the bibliography of a subject begins with the first essay they have devoted to it. Although the past of Egyptology is so short, it is a difficult subject to know, and it is not surprising if Bissing has misrepresented some features or ignored others. For example, he attributes the merit of recognizing in the animal's tail that the kings attach to their back, not

Studies in Egyptian Art

a lion's tail but a jackal's * to Wiedemann; I do not know if I was the first, but I think that I certainly stated this before Wiedemann.† A little farther on, I regret that Bissing was not acquainted with my notice of the statue of Montouhotpou in the *Musée Egyptien* :‡ I am curious to know if he accepts my explanation of the disproportion between the feet, legs, and bust. It seems to me that it was not intended to be on the same level as the spectator, but that it ought to be placed in a naos, on a fairly high platform which could be reached by a staircase in front : seen from below, foreshortened, the effect of the perspective would redeem the exaggeration of form and re-establish the balance between the parts. It seems also that Bissing was not acquainted with the part of the *Musée* in which this Montouhotpou is discussed, for he does not refer to it again with regard to the Amenemhaît III discovered by Flinders Petrie at Fayoum. § Farther on again, it would have been in keeping to note that Legrain found the debris of a statuette in black granite in the mud of the *favissa* at Karnak, which so closely resembles the admirable Ramses II of Turin that it might almost be the replica or a sort of original rough model. ǁ Unfortunately the head is wanting, but we have been almost entirely successful in restoring the body: if it is not by the same sculptor who took such pleasure in modelling the Turin statue, it comes from the same royal studio. The few

* Bissing, II. *Plate with the name of King Athotis*, note 6.

† I even noted the existence of one of these tails in wood in the Marseilles Museum (*Catalogue*, p. 92, No. 279).

‡ *Musée Egyptien*, vol. ii., Pl. IX–X and pp. 25–30.

§ Ibid., vol. ii., Pl. XV, pp. 41–45.

ǁ Maspero, *Guide to the Cairo Museum*, 1906, pp. 156–7, No. 550.

Egyptian Statuary

differences to be noted between them arise solely from the inequality of the stature: it was necessary to simplify certain details or to suppress them in the smallest of the statues.

These examples show that there is nothing very serious in the omissions and negligences: we are surprised not that there should be some, but that among such a mass of references there are not more. I might perhaps disagree with some of the theories or points of doctrine Bissing constantly advances, but I will wait to do so until he has elaborated into a system the elements so abundantly spread through the notices. But there is one criticism I will make now: he scarcely mentions the schools into which Egypt was divided, so that we are tempted to conclude that, like so many contemporary archæologists, he believes in the existence of one sole school, which worked in an almost uniform manner over the whole of Egypt at one time. It is, however, certain that there were always several schools on the banks of the Nile, each of which possessed its traditions, its designs, its method of interpreting the costume or the pose of individuals, the works of which have a sufficiently special physiognomy to admit of their being easily separated into their different groups. Here, again, it seems to me that sometimes varieties of execution which are the result of the teaching are taken to be signs of age, and that pieces which are contemporary within a few years, but which proceed from distinct schools, are spread over centuries. I have not discovered Bissing in such errors: his natural insight and his knowledge of the monuments preserved him from making them. I wish, however, that he had touched on the matter more definitely than he has, and, after letting it

Studies in Egyptian Art

be seen in several places that he admits the existence of those schools, he should have defined their characteristics in accordance as the progress of his book brought their work before the reader. He has briefly touched on the matter in regard to the sphinxes of Tanis and the statue of Amenemhaît III, but he might, for example, have seized the opportunity of the Montouhotpou in order to demonstrate the tendencies of Theban art at its birth; he could have followed them in their evolution, and the Amenôthes I of Turin might perhaps have served to teach us how those tendencies were developed or modified between the beginning of the first Theban Empire and that of the second. A passage in the notice of the so-called Hyksôs sphinxes leads me to hope that he will do this for the Tanite school in regard to the celebrated *Bearers of offerings*: I greatly wish that I may not be disappointed in my hope.

III

As far as I can judge there were at least four large schools of sculpture in the valley of the Nile: at Memphis, Thebes, Hermopolis, and in the eastern part of the delta. I have attempted farther on to sketch the history and define the principal characteristics of the Theban school;[*] I shall only refer to it as far as it is necessary to make clear in what it is distinguished from the three others.

And to begin with, it is probable that the first of those in date, the Memphian, is merely the prolongation and continuation of a previous Thinite school. If I

[*] *Revue de l'Art Ancien et Moderne*, 1906, vol. x., pp. 241-52, 337-48; cf. Chap. X. of the present volume.

Egyptian Statuary

compare the few objects of real art that have come to us from the Thinites with parallel works of which the necropolises of Gizeh, Saqqarah and the Fayoum have restored to us so many examples, I am struck by the resemblances in inspiration and technique that exist between the two. We have no statues originating from Thinis itself, but the stelæ, the amulets in alto-relievo, the fragments of minute furniture discovered in the tombs of Omm-el-Gaâb find their exact counterpart in similar pieces that come from the excavations of Abousîr-el-Malak or of Meîdoum and from the sub-structure of Memphian residences. I think I see that at the beginning there were mediocre workmen in the plain of the Pyramids capable, however, of sculpturing, ill or well, a statue of a man seated or standing: to those men I attribute the statue No. 1 in the Cairo Museum, the Matonou (Amten) of Berlin, the Sapoui (Sepa) of the Louvre, and a few other lesser ones. The same defects are to be seen in all: the head out of proportion to the body, the neck ungraceful, the shoulders high, the bust summarily rough-hewn and without regard to the dimensions of each part, the arms and legs heavy, thick, angular. Their roughness and awkwardness compared with the beautiful appearance of the two statues of Meîdoum, which are almost contemporary with them, would astonish us if we did not think that the latter, commissioned for relatives of Sanofraouî, proceed from the royal workshops. The transference of the capital to Memphis, or rather to the district stretching from the entrance into the Fayoum to the fork of the delta, necessarily resulted in impoverishing Thinis-Abydos; the stone-cutters, architects, statuaries, and masons aecompanied the court, and planted the traditions and teaching

Studies in Egyptian Art

of their respective fatherlands in their new homes. According to what is seen in the tombs of Meîdoum, the latest Thinite style, or rather the transition style of the IIIrd Dynasty, presents exactly the same characteristics as the perfect style of the IVth, Vth, and VIth Dynasties, but with a less stiff manner. The pose of the persons and the silhouettes of the animals are already schematized and encircled in the lines which will enclose them almost to the end of Egyptian civilization, but the detail is freer, and keeps very close to reality. The tendency is perceived only in the roundness and suppleness that prevails from the time of Cheops and Chephrên. The Memphites sought to idealize their models rather than to make a faithful copy of them, and while respecting the general resemblance, desired to give the spectator an impression of calm majesty or of gentleness. Their manner was adopted at Thinis by a counter-shock, and it may be said that from the IVth to the XXVIth Dynasty Abydos remained almost a branch of the Memphian school, which, however, grew out of it. The productions only differ from those of the Memphites in subordinate points, except during the XIXth Dynasty, when Setouî I and Ramses II summoned Theban sculptors there, and for some years it became, artistically, a fief of Thebes.

If we would indicate in one word the character of this Thinito-Memphian art, we should say that it resides in an idealism of convention as opposed to the realism of Theban art. Thanks to the fluctuations of political life which alternately made Memphis and Thebes the capitals of the whole kingdom, the æsthetics of the two cities spread to the neighbouring towns, and did not allow them to form an independent art: Heracleopolis, Beni-

Egyptian Statuary

Hassan, Assiout, Abydos took after Memphis, while the Said and Nubia, from Denderah to Napata, remained under the jurisdiction of Thebes. An original school arose, however, in one place, and persisted for a fairly long time, in Hermopolis Magna, the city of Thot. We observe there, from the end of the Ancient Empire, sculptors who devoted themselves to expressing with a scrupulous naturalism, and often with an intentional seeking after ugliness, the bearing of individuals and the movement of groups. We should observe with what humour they interpreted the extremes of obesity and emaciation in man and beast, in the two tombs called *the fat and the lean*. The region where they flourished is so little explored that it is still unknown how long their activity practised a continuous style: it was at its best under the first Theban Empire, at Bercheh, at Beni-Hassan, at Cheikh-Said, but the period at which it seems to me to be most in evidence was at the end of the XVIIIth Dynasty, under the heretic Pharaohs. When Amenôthes IV founded his capital of Khouîtatonou, if, as is probable, he settled some Theban masters there, he would certainly have utilized the studios of Hermopolis. The scenes engraved on the tombs of El-Tell and El-Amarna are due to the same spirit and the same teaching as those of the *fat and lean* tombs; there are similar deformations of the human figure bordering on caricature, the same suppleness and sometimes the same violence in the gestures and attitudes. In a number of portraits the Theban importation prevails, but the cavalcades, processions, royal audiences, popular scenes, must be attributed to the Hermopolitans, for their inspiration and execution present so striking a contrast to those of analogous pictures that adorn the walls of Louxor or Karnak. The fall of the little Atonian Dynasty stopped their activity;

Studies in Egyptian Art

deprived of the vast commissions which opened a new field for their enterprise, they fell back into their provincial routine, and we have not yet enough documents to tell us what their successors became in the course of the centuries.

In the delta two fairly different styles may be seen from the beginning. In the east, at Tanis and in its neighbourhood, there is, at the beginning of the first Theban Empire, a veritable school, the productions of which possess such an individual physiognomy that Mariette did not hesitate to attribute them to the Shepherd Kings: since the works of Golenischeff it is known that the so-called Hyksôs sphinxes are of Amenemhaît III, and that they belong to the second half of the XIIth Dynasty. This Tanite school is perpetuated through the ages; it was still flourishing under the XXIst and XXIInd Dynasties, as is proved by the fine group of bearers of offerings in the Cairo Museum. The predominant features are the energy and harshness of the modelling, especially of the human face: its masters have copied a type, and modes of coiffure belonging, as Mariette formerly pointed out, to the half-savage populations of Lake Menzaleh, the *Egyptians in the marshes* of Herodotus. It seems to me that their manner is still to be noted in the Græco-Roman period in the statues of princes and priests that we have in the Cairo Museum: the technical skill, however, is less than in the sphinxes and the bearers of offerings. The centre and west of the delta, on the other hand, came under the influence of Memphis, as far as we can judge from the rare existing fragments belonging to the Ancient Empire. Under the Thebans the dependence is clear, and all that comes from those regions differs in nothing from what we have from the Memphian necropolises.

Egyptian Statuary

Only in the Ethiopian period, and under the influence of the successors of Bocchoris, is a Saïte school revealed to us, which, borrowing its general composition from the Memphian school, comes closer to nature and impresses an individual stamp on certain elements of the human figure that until then had been handled in a loose, so to say, an abstract fashion. The modelling of the face is as full of expression as in the fine works of the Theban school, but with greater finish and less harsh effects; the ravages of old age, wrinkles, crows'-feet, flabbiness of flesh, thinness, are all reproduced with a care unusual in preceding generations; the skull, indeed, is so minute in detail that it might almost be called an anatomical study. This impulse towards skilled realism, begun by instinct in the heart of the school, became accentuated and accelerated by contact with the Hellenes, who from the time of Psammetichus I swarmed in the provinces of the delta. Certain bas-reliefs of Alexandria and Cairo, the date of which is assigned to the reign of Nectanebo II, which I should like to place in that of one of the first Ptolemies,* may be regarded as extant witnesses of a kind of composite art analogous to that which was developed two centuries later at Alexandria or at Memphis, and of which the Cairo Museum possesses some rare examples.

It should be clearly understood that I do not claim to put the complete result of my study of the schools, the presence of which in Ancient Egypt is now confirmed, in these few lines. I am only anxious to point out the part played by them in historic times, and the errors into which those who have written the history of Egyptian art without suspecting their existence, or without taking into consideration what we do know of them,

* *Musée Egyptien*, vol. ii., pp. 90–2.

Studies in Egyptian Art

have fallen. Bissing does not ignore them, and is doubtless waiting to criticize them in his Introduction. He has so much material that it will be easy for him to rectify my hypotheses, and to confirm them where necessary; in that way his book will gain by being no longer a mere collection of monuments each described as an isolated piece, but a veritable treatise on sculpture, or at least on Egyptian statuary.

I shall be sincerely sorry if he fails in that particular, but even so, I should feel it right to declare that he has come honourably out of an enterprise in which he had no predecessors. The few plates that I inserted a quarter of a century ago in the *Monuments de l'Art Antique,* and the notices contained in the parts of the *Musée Egyptien* that have already appeared, afforded both experts and amateurs a foretaste of the surprises that Egypt has in store in the matter of art; they have been too few, and have related to subjects too scattered in point of time, to produce a body of doctrine. But here, on the contrary, nearly two hundred pieces are available, classified according to the order of the Dynasties, and for the most part unpublished, or better reproduced than in the past. Each will be accompanied by an analysis in which the researches previously connected with it will be set forth and discussed; for the first time Egyptologists and the general public will have the artistic and critical apparatus required for judging the value of the principal pieces of Egyptian statuary before their eyes and in their hands. Those who know the amount of the literature existing on Egyptology, and how scattered it is, can easily imagine the patience and bibliographical *flair* that Bissing must have needed for gathering from libraries the information so generously scattered on every page of his notices. But that was

Egyptian Statuary

only the least part of his task; the appreciation of the objects themselves demanded of him an ever alert attention and a continuous tension of mind which would promptly have exhausted a man less devoted to the minutiæ of artistic observation. In other branches of the science, the materials have for the most part been so often and so repeatedly kneaded that nearly always half of the work has been already done; here, nothing of that sort exists, and in many cases Bissing has dealt with objects that he was the first to know, and of which no previous study had been attempted. That he is sometimes weary, and that here and there his opinions may be controverted, he willingly confesses. But what surprises me is how very rarely it is necessary to upset them, even partially.

I hope then that we shall not have to wait too long for the completion of this admirable work. May I venture to add that after the present edition, which is an *édition de luxe*, a popular edition would be welcome? Egyptologists like myself are condemned to pay such large sums for our books that the price of these "Denkmäler" does not alarm us, but the fact has greater importance for others. A reproduction in a smaller *format*, and less expensive, would greatly help to spread the knowledge of Egyptian art among classes of readers whom the book in its present form will not reach.

II

SOME PORTRAITS OF MYCERINUS*

IT has long been a debatable question if the Egyptian statues of kings and private individuals can be regarded as faithful portraits or as merely approximate to their originals. No one has ever denied that their authors desired to make them as like as possible, but we hesitate to believe that they succeeded in doing so. The air of uniformity lent them by the repeated employment of the same expressions and the same postures encouraged the notion that, judging themselves incapable of exactly transcribing the details of bodily form or physiognomy proper to each individual, the sculptors decided that such details were not necessary for the kind of service to which the statues were destined: they considered that the task entrusted to them was sufficiently fulfilled if the soul or the *double* for which these statues provided an imperishable body recognized in them enough of the perishable body to enable them to attach themselves to it without hurt in the course of their posthumous existence. The study of the monuments has dissipated those doubts. Any one who has carefully handled one of the Saïte heads, the skull and face of which present such clearly individual characteristics, must acknowledge that so many details noted with such felicitous care indicate

* From the *Revue de l'Art ancien et moderne*, 1912, vol. xxxi., pp. 241-54.

Some Portraits of Mycerinus

an absolute intention of transmitting the exact appearance of the model to posterity. And if, proceeding forward, we reach the second Theban period, we shall soon, thanks to the chances which have delivered to us the well-preserved corpses of about fifty princes and princesses, recognize the success with which the royal studios perpetuated in stone the effigies of their contemporaries. The profile of Setouî I photographed in his coffin would coincide line for line with that of his bas-reliefs of Karnak or Abydos were it not for the thinness resulting from embalmment. Let us go back eight or ten centuries and see how the master sculptors of the first Theban period treated their Pharaohs. The statues of Amenemhaît III and of Sanouosrît have so personal a note that we should be wrong to imagine they could be anything but a sincere, almost a brutal likeness. The two Chephrên of the Cairo Museum were not long ago alone in suggesting to us the conviction that the Memphian times yielded nothing in this matter of resemblance to ages farther removed from us; the recent discovery of ten statues of Mycerinus prevents any further doubt.

Most of them have not left Egypt. The first that came to us was acquired by purchase in 1888, with four statuettes of Naousirrîya, of Mankahorou, of Chephrên, and perhaps of Cheops. According to the information collected at the time by Grébaut, they were found together, two or three weeks before, by fellahs of Mit-Rahineh under the ruins of a little brick building situated at the east of what was formerly the sacred lake of the temple of Phtah at Memphis. That was certainly not their original place; they had probably each adorned first the funerary chapel annexed to the pyramid of its sovereign: their transference to the town and their reunion in the place where they were discovered are not earlier than the reign of the last Saïtes

Studies in Egyptian Art

or the first Ptolemies. It was then, in fact, that hatred of foreign domination having exalted the love of all that was peculiarly Egyptian in the eyes of the people, reverence for the glorious Pharaohs of former ages revived: their priesthoods were reorganized, and they again received the worship to which centuries of neglect had disaccustomed them. None of our figures are life-size, and the Mycerinus in diorite, which is not one of the smallest, is scarcely $21\frac{1}{8}$ inches in height. It is enthroned on a cubical block with the impassibility that the Chephrên has made familiar to us; the bust is stiff, the arms rest on the thighs, he looks straight before him, his face expressionless, as was imposed on Pharaoh by etiquette, while the crowd of courtiers and vassals filed past at his feet: if his name, engraved on the sides of his seat to the right and left of his legs, had not told who he was, we should have guessed it from his bearing. The composition, although not the best imaginable, is good: but the head makes a poor effect in relation to the torso, a defect always at first ascribed to the heedlessness of the sculptor. But it is to be noted that the face somewhat recalled that of two of the other Pharaohs, a fact to be explained by the relationship, the second, Chephrên, being the father of Mycerinus, and the third, probably Cheops, his grandfather. That is a reason for presuming that they are portraits, but are they authentic portraits? Several Berlin Egyptologists whose natural ingenuity encouraged them to revise Mariette's criticisms on art, thought to discern in certain details of the costume and ornamentation a proof that if they were not figures of pure imagination, they were at least copies of ancient originals freely executed under one of the Saïte Dynasties, and their theory, although opposed by experts who had a longer experience, disconcerted the majority. It was soon upset by facts, but, as

THE **MYCERINUS** OF MÎT-RAHINEH.
Diorite. Cairo Museum.

Some Portraits of Mycerinus

often happens, the consequences deduced from it survived by force of habit. Many of us feared for some years after to be asserting too much, to declare openly that our Mycerinus was what we had entitled him on the faith of his inscription, the real Mycerinus.

We did not do so until 1908, when Reisner and his Americans, excavating at Gizeh round about the third pyramid, brought to light monuments that with the best will in the world no one could assign to any other epoch than that of Mycerinus. It seems that the fame of piety which popular story ascribed to him was not wholly unmerited, at least as far as his own divinity is concerned, for with the elements of a voluminous funerary equipment in all kinds of stones, the workmen brought out of the ruins of the chapel, fragments of a multitude of statues in alabaster, schist, limestone, and rare breccia. Among them were some unfinished or scarcely shaped out, for the sovereign having died while they were being fashioned, the works, according to Oriental custom, had been immediately interrupted and the workshops abandoned in confusion.

The statues which were already finished and set up in their places were overturned at some unknown period, perhaps when Saladin dismantled the pyramids to build the new ramparts and citadel of Cairo, and the fragments were so ill-treated that an enormous number of them have disappeared. Out of a hundred baskets of debris collected by the Americans, they found at most, besides five or six intact heads, enough to put together, almost completely, two alabaster statues. The best of the heads is in the Cairo Museum, and it has sufficient resemblance to our statuette for us to have no hesitation in recognizing Mycerinus, even if the place whence it comes did not help us to guess it. The statue that the find

Studies in Egyptian Art

brought us is seated, but the block on which it is sculptured is not perpendicular to its base, so that it leans slightly backward. On the other hand, the two arms being cut between the armpit and the hip, the accident makes it appear at first glance as if the bust is too narrow for its height. But, and this is the important point, the head is small, so small that the head-dress, in spite of its size, is not sufficient to correct the bad effect of this disproportion between its smallness and the amplitude of the shoulders. The fault is not to be ascribed to the artist's ignorance and lack of skill, as is probably done. He was not, it must be admitted, a man of talent, but he knew his business, and proved it by the general quality of his work. The harmony between the trunk and the leg, the muscles of the chest, the texture of the costume, the modelling of the knee and calf, conform to the æsthetics of the time; the foot and ankle are particularized with the virtuosity of a craftsman skilled in all the subtleties of his calling. So, now, returning to the statuette of Mit-Rahineh, the technique of which shows it to proceed not from a different school but from a different studio, we shall find a difficulty in imagining that two sculptors would each have fallen into so great an error, if they had not seen it themselves in their model. Since their statues are microcephalous, Mycerinus must have been microcephalous almost to deformity.

The search among the beds of fragments of stone was continued. A few weeks before it was finished, at the end of May, 1908, it produced four groups in schist, the testimony of which fully confirmed that of the alabaster statues. The disposition is the same, with very slight divergences, which do not sensibly modify the aspect of the pieces. Three persons stand side by side against a

ALABASTER STATUE OF MYCERINUS
Cairo Museum.

Some Portraits of Mycerinus

slab 17 to 23 inches high. Mycerinus is in the middle, his left foot advanced, the waist-cloth fluted on the loins, and on his forehead the white cap of the kingdom of Upper Egypt. He always has a goddess on his right, a Hathor moulded in the sleeveless smock open on the chest, and on her hair the short wig and the *coufieh*. On the top of this head-dress she wears her two cow's horns and the solar disk. In one of the groups she is walking, her arms hanging down and her hands laid flat on her thighs; in the second, she embraces him with her left arm and presses against him; in the third she holds his right hand in her left. The last of the figures is sometimes a woman, sometimes a man: the man, who is shorter by a third than his companions, walks forward swinging his arms; the two women are at rest, and one of them puts her right arm round the king's waist, in symmetry with the Hathor on the left. They are geographical entities, nomes, and the standards on their heads tell us their names: the two women personify the nomes of Sistrum and the Dog, the man that of Oxyrrhinchus. The fragments of schist under which they were buried assuredly belong to other groups now destroyed, but how many of them were there in the beginning? The decorative theme of which they formed part is one of which the intention is grasped at the first glance, but if we needed a commentary to explain it, the brief legends at the base would provide the material. They inform us, in fact, that our Hathor is the lady of the Canton of the Sycomore, and that the nome of the Dog, that of the Sistrum, that of Oxyrrhinchus, bring the sovereign all the good things of their territory. Mycerinus, in his quality of king of the Said and of the delta, had a right to tribute during his life, and to offerings after his

Studies in Egyptian Art

death from the whole country, and on the other hand, Hathor, lady of the Sycomore, is the patron of dead Osirians in the Memphian province where the palaces and tombs of the Pharaohs are. It was natural then that she should serve as the introducer of the delegates of the nomes when they came to pay their tribute to the common master. With rich private individuals, the operation was symbolized on the walls of the funerary chapels by long processions of men or women in bas-relief, each of whom incarnated one of the domains charged with the upkeep of the tomb. Here it was expressed in even a more concrete fashion by two series of groups in rondo-bosso, which were probably developed on the walls in one of the court-yards of the temple of the pyramid. The four which have escaped destruction belonged to the series of the Said, as is proved by their names and the head-dress of the sovereign, but those of the delta could not have been omitted without causing regrettable privations to the *double* in his life beyond the tomb; there were then about forty in all, as many as there were nomes in the whole of Egypt.

The excellence of those that have survived fills us with regret for those that are lost. At the instant they emerged from the earth, they preserved something of their primitive colouring, but contact with the air and light speedily deprived them of it, and only traces remain on the chest, at the neck, wrists, waist, places protected by the customary ornaments of people of high rank. The gold-leaf with which the necklaces and bracelets were decorated was stolen in times of antiquity, but the thicker layers of paint on which they were placed preserve their contours fairly exactly. It would be easy for us to restore to the whole the aspect it had

MYCERINUS, HATHOR, AND THE NOME OXYRRHINCHUS.

Some Portraits of Mycerinus

when fresh and new—a light yellow complexion for the women, and red-brown for the men, black hair, blue or white head-dresses, white crowns, and garments relieved by the tawny brilliance of the jewels. In pieces where everything is so minutely calculated for reality, it is scarcely probable that anything is the effect of chance or of lack of skill; if then the sovereign's head is too small it is because it was so in reality. In fact, the lack of proportion with the rest of the body is less perceptible here than in the isolated statues, and it is not perceptible at the first glance: but it is soon recognized when the sovereign is compared with his two companions. Not only are their heads larger and more massive than his, but it would seem that the sculptor desired to accentuate the inequality between them by a trick of his craft: he has perceptibly narrowed their shoulders, and the contrast between the small head that surmounts the vast shoulders of Mycerinus with the two large heads that weight the narrow shoulders of the acolytes, emphasizes the deformity that the placing together of three figures on the same level had almost concealed. Study of the schists leads to the same conclusion as that formed of the alabasters. It is the real Mycerinus that contemporaries have bound themselves to transmit to posterity, and they have spared no details which were naturally calculated to make us better acquainted with him. We have only to analyse their works to see him stand before us in his habit as he lived. He was tall, robust, slender, with long legs, powerful shoulders surmounted by a small face, an athlete with the head almost of a child. In addition, projecting eyes, big ears, a short nose, the tip turned up, a sensual mouth with full lips, a chin receding under the artificial beard; the expression of the

Studies in Egyptian Art

face is benevolent, even weak. In vain has the sculptor stiffened the backbone and the neck, thrown out the chest, stretched the biceps, clenched the fist, and immobilized the features into a hieratic gravity: he has not succeeded in inculcating the sovereign majesty that makes our Chephrên the ideal Pharaoh, the equal of the gods. He has the sanctimonious appearance of a private individual of good family, but his general bearing is below his condition. We could easily point to a dozen statues, his neighbours in the Cairo Museum, that of Rânafir, for instance, which have a more exalted appearance and a prouder mien.

And the new schist group that Reisner discovered during the winter of 1909 has not made any change in our opinion necessary. This time Mycerinus is represented with his wife; the lower portions of the two figures had not received the final polish when death intervened, but those of the upper part were finished and are admirable. Mycerinus wears the head-dress of the ordinary *claft*, which squarely frames the face, and his features are those with which we have become familiar in the statues described above; eyes starting from his head, a fixed expression, turned up nose, a large, loose mouth, the lower lip protruding, the physiognomy of a man of the middle class straining to appear dignified. The queen does not appear much more noble, but in looking at her we are disposed to think that she had more intelligence and vivacity. We should not say that she was exactly smiling, but a smile has just passed over her face, and traces of it remain on her lips and in her eyes. She has beautiful round cheeks, a little turned-up nose, a full chin, full lips cleft from top to bottom by a strongly

MYCERINUS AND HIS WIFE.
Schist. Boston Museum

Some Portraits of Mycerinus

marked furrow: a determined expression shows itself between her narrow, heavy eyelids. She resembles her husband, a fact that is not surprising, since unions between brothers and sisters were not only tolerated but commanded by custom; there is thus every chance that the couple were born of the same father and mother; she has only a greater appearance of strength than he has. Custom exacted that, when a husband and wife were associated in a group, they should not be placed side by side on a level of absolute equality, but that the woman should be given a posture or merely a gesture implying a state of more or less affectionate dependence on the husband; she crouched at his feet, her chest against his knees, or her arm was round his waist or his neck, as if she had no trust except in his protection. Here the queen's gesture is in conformity with convention, but the manner of its execution contradicts the intention of submission: she leans less against the Pharaoh than she draws him close to her, and looks as if she is protecting him at least as much as he is protecting her. She is his equal in height, and even if she is more slender than he is, as is proper to her sex, her shoulders are as robust. Does it mean that the sculptor has attributed to her the massive shoulders of a man? Not at all: but following the example of his colleagues in the triads, he has cheated a little in order to dissimulate the defect of his model. As doubtless he would not have liked to show a deformed Pharaoh, and as he might not alter features which, after all, were those of a god, he has made the deformity less visible by taking away from the shoulders what was wanted in order to establish a sort of apparent equilibrium between the parts, and so we are brought

Studies in Egyptian Art

back by a fresh detour to the point to which the examination of the alabasters and triads had led us. Let us once more conclude that the effigies of the Memphian Pharaohs and their subjects were real portraits of the personages they claimed to reproduce.

They were real, but not realistic unless there was special necessity. I have repeatedly attempted to define the two chief schools of Egyptian sculpture, the Theban and the Memphian. From the beginning the Theban school tends to copy the model brutally, as it was at the moment when it was portrayed. Take the statues of Sanouosrît I or of Sanouosrît III, which lately came to the Cairo Museum. The family likeness between all of them is indubitable, but, according as they come from a Theban or Memphian studio, the features which constitute the complete resemblance are noted in such divergent ways that at the first glance we are inclined to think that it scarcely exists. The Thebans scrupulously marked the thinness of the cheeks, the hardness of the eye, the harshness of the mouth, the heaviness of the jaw, and have exaggerated rather than diminished those points. The Memphians do not neglect them, but have treated them in a more merciful manner, and, from the haggard faces in which the rival school took pleasure, have brought out the happy smiling expression that its own traditions ascribed without exception to all the Pharaohs. We cannot institute comparisons of that kind for the epoch of Mycerinus: the Theban school, if, as is probable, it was then in existence, still sleeps buried beneath the ruins, and we know nothing belonging to it to place by the side of the Memphian. It is sufficient, however, to walk through the rooms of the Cairo Museum reserved for it to be convinced that if the Cheîkh-el-Beled, the Chephrên statues, the royal couple of Meîdoum, the Rânafir statues are portraits and likenesses, they are at the

MYCERINUS, HATHOR, AND THE NOME OF THE SISTRUM.

Schist. Cairo Museum

Some Portraits of Mycerinus

same time idealized portraits according to the formula, the influence of which we have seen in the monuments of the XIIth Dynasty. Whatever the models presented that was too pronounced, was softened in order to give them the serene bearing fitting the imperishable bodies of such noble and respectable persons. They only departed from this routine when there were monstrosities, the entire suppression of which would have been fraught with danger for the immortality of the subject, as in the case of the two dwarfs in the Cairo Museum ; but it is not quite certain if even in those cases some modification of the ugliness has not been contrived. What has happened to Mycerinus renders it probable: have we not seen, in fact, that the artist exerted his ingenuity to dissimulate the disturbing exiguity of the head by an artifice? And he must often have taken similar liberties, although we have no actual means of proving it. I will venture to assert it of Chephrên, although almost the half of one of his two statues, that in green serpentine, is a restoration by Vassalli. For if we compare their profiles, we notice that that of the serpentine statue is weaker than that of the diorite statue: the eye is smaller and the chin less authoritative, the tip of the nose recedes a little, and there is a slight resemblance with Mycerinus. The lofty dignity which I noted just now as appearing in the father in contrast to the son may be the result of the Memphians' determination to idealize their subjects so as to make each of them an almost abstract type of the class to which they belonged.

As might be expected, the alabasters of Mycerinus are a long way from equalling the schists. Indeed, whenever we find statues of a person in different materials, it is seldom that those most difficult to work in are not also the best. Petrie concluded that in all periods Egypt had a school of sculpture in limestone and soft stones,

Studies in Egyptian Art

and one in granite and hard stones. But who would think of classifying modern sculptors in different schools according as they used bronze or marble? In Egypt, as in later times, the instruction given to learners prepared them to practise the complete calling, whatever the special branch to which they later confined themselves might be, but as the handling of certain stones required a more extended practice, care was taken in the workshops to entrust them to the most expert. That is evidently what happened in the case of Mycerinus. His alabasters are certainly very estimable; but those to whom we owe them were not skilled virtuosi, and if they acquitted themselves of their task honourably, they only produced ordinary work. Those who executed the schists were much more skilled. I will not venture to assert that they entirely triumphed over their material: the bodies of princes and gods sculptured in matter so unyielding and of so gloomy a tone present a rigidity of contour which we feel as keenly as we do the lack of colour which would enliven them. They almost repel any one who sees them for the first time, but the repulsion once overcome, they reveal themselves as perfect of their kind. The artist has done what he wished with the ungrateful material, and has handled it with the same suppleness as if he had been kneading the most ductile clay. The women are especially remarkable with their full round shoulders, their small breasts placed low, the belly strong and well designed, the thighs full and graceful, the legs vigorous, one of the most elegant types created by Memphian Egypt. It does not equal the diorite Chephrên, nor the Cheîkh-el-Beled, nor the Crouching Scribe, nor the lady of Meîdoum, but it is not so far removed from them, and few pieces take so high a rank in the work of the old Memphian school.

MYCERINUS AND HIS WIFE (DETAIL).
Schist. Boston Museum.

III

A SCRIBE'S HEAD
OF THE IVTH OR VTH DYNASTY

(*The Louvre*)

THE inventories give no indication of the origin of this head. So little was its source suspected that for a long time it was believed to be of Peruvian work : M. de Longpérier with his usual tact restored it to its rightful place in the Egyptian series.* At the first glance the style is seen to be that of the ancient Memphian Empire : it has evidently been detached from a statue found in one of the necropolises of Saqqarah. The absence of the plinth and the parts which usually bear the inscription prevents us from knowing the name of the individual it represents, a scribe contemporary, or very nearly, with the celebrated Crouching Scribe. A narrow and somewhat receding forehead, a long prominent eye slightly drawn up towards the temples, snub-nose, thin nostrils, accentuated cheekbones, thin cheeks, large mouth with full lips, a firm rounded chin, do not make a flattering portrait but certainly an exact one. The material is the excellent limestone of Tourah painted bright red : the technique

---

* It is mentioned for the first time in Emmanuel de Rougé's *Catalogue*, 1855, under No. 6 ; it is placed on the mantelpiece in the " Salle civile."

Studies in Egyptian Art

shows delicacy and skill rare even at that period of admirable artists.

Almost all the statues of mere private individuals come from temples or tombs. The right of setting up a statue in the temples belonged exclusively to the king; so the greater number of those we have offer a special formula: "*Granted as a favour* on the part of the king to a son of so and so,"* sometimes too the favour is qualified as *great* or *very great*. It was then by some exceptional title, in reward of services rendered, or by a caprice of royalty, that an Egyptian was authorized to place his portrait in a temple, whether of his native city or of some other town, to the god for whom he professed a special devotion. The great feudal lords, who all more or less aspired to possess royal rights, sometimes took the liberty of setting up a statue of themselves without the preliminary permission of Pharaoh; but in spite of these usurpations of the royal prerogative, the number is relatively small. Civil wars, foreign invasions, the ruin of towns, the destruction of idols by the Christians, contributed to make private statues coming from temples rare in our museums.†

But, on the other hand, those that come from cemeteries are very numerous. Every tomb that was somewhat cared for in the ancient or new empire contained several which represented the defunct alone, or accompanied by the principal members of his family. They were not always placed in the same spot: in the IVth Dynasty they were sometimes placed in the outer court, in the

---

* See good examples in Mariette, " Karnak," Pl. VIII.

† This is no longer true since the discovery of the *favissa* at Karnak. The Cairo Museum possesses some hundreds of statues of private individuals from the Theban temple of Amon (1912).

SCRIBE'S HEAD.
The Louvre.

A Scribe's Head

open air, sometimes also in the chapel, where on certain days the family celebrated the worship of the ancestor. Most often they were imprisoned in a narrow chamber, with a lofty ceiling, something like a corridor, and for that reason called *Serdâb* by the Arabs. Sometimes the *Serdâb* is lost in the masonry and does not communicate with any of the other chambers. Sometimes it is connected with the funerary chapel by a sort of quadrangular pipe, so small that a hand can scarcely be inserted.* The priests would burn incense near the orifice, pour libations, present offerings, murmur prayers, and everything was supposed to penetrate to the little apartment. Some of these *Serdâb* contained one or two statues at most, others would contain twenty. Some are in wood or hard stone, but the greater number are in painted limestone. Seated or standing, crouching or in the attitude of walking, they all claim to be portraits—portraits of the dead man, of his wife, of his children, of his servants. If they were more often found in places where they would have been visible, their presence would be explained by the pleasure members of a family would feel in seeing the features of those they had loved. But they are generally walled up for all eternity in hidden corners where no one would ever penetrate: we must seek other reasons.

The Egyptians formed a somewhat coarse idea of the human soul. They regarded it as an exact reproduction of the body of each individual, formed of a substance less dense than flesh and bones, but susceptible to the sight, feeling, and touch. The *double,* or to call it by the name they gave it, the *ka,* was subject, though in a lesser

* Mariette, "Sur les tombes de l'Ancien Empire qu'on trouve à Saqqarah," 1912, pp. 8–9.

Studies in Egyptian Art

degree than its terrestrial type, to all the infirmities of our life: it drank, ate, clothed itself, anointed itself with perfumes, came and went in its tomb, required furniture, a house, servants, an income. A man must be assured beyond the tomb of the possession of all the wealth he had enjoyed in the world, under penalty of being condemned to an eternity of unspeakable misery. His family's first obligation towards him was to provide him with a durable body; they therefore mummified his mortal remains to the best of their ability, and buried the mummy at the bottom of a pit where it could only be reached with the greatest difficulty. The body, however, in spite of the care taken in preparing it, only very remotely recalled the form of the living person. It was, besides, unique and easily destroyed: it could be broken, methodically dismembered, and the pieces scattered or burnt. If it disappeared, what would become of the *double*? For its support statues were provided, representing the exact form of the individual. Effigies in wood, limestone, hard stone, bronze, were more solid than the mummy, and there was nothing to prevent the manufacture of any number of them desired. One body was a single chance of durability for the *double*: twenty gave it twenty chances. And that is the explanation of the astonishing number of statues sometimes found in one tomb. The piety of the relatives multiplied the images, and consequently the supports, the imperishable bodies, of the *double* would, by themselves alone, almost assure him immortality.*

---

* On this theory see Lepage-Renouf, "On the True Sense of an important Egyptian Word," in the *Transactions of the Society of Biblical Archæology*, vol. iv., pp. 494-508, and Maspero, "Mémoires du Congrès des Orientalistes de Lyon," vol. i., and *Bulletin de l'Association scientifique de France* (1878), No. 594, pp. 373-84.

A Scribe's Head

Both in the temples and hypogeums, the statues of private persons were intended to serve as a support to the soul. The consecration they received animated them, so to speak, and made them substitutes for the defunct: the offerings destined for the other world were served to them. The tomb of a rich man possessed a veritable chapel to which a special body of priests was attached, formed of *hon-ka* or *priests of the double*. At the sacramental festivals the *priests of the double* performed the necessary rites, they looked after the upkeep of the edifice and administered its revenues. The statues of the towns themselves demanded particular care. Indeed, the clergy of the temple in which they were placed claimed their part in the advantages derived from ancestor worship: veritable acts of donation were drawn up in their favour, in which were specified the part they were to play in the ceremonies, the quantity of the offerings that fell to their share for the service rendered, the number of days in the year consecrated to each statue. " Agreement between Prince Hapi-T'aufi and the *hour-priests* of the temple of Anubis, master of Siout, in regard to one white loaf that each must give to the statue of the prince, under the hand of the *ka-priest*, the 18th Thot, the day of the festival of *Ouaga*,* and also the gifts which every tomb owes to its lord; afterwards in regard to the ceremony of kindling the flame, and the procession that they ought to make with the *ka-priest* while he celebrates the service in honour of the defunct, and that they march to the north corner of the temple on the day of kindling the flame. For that Hapi-T'aufi gives the *hour-priests* a bushel of corn from each of the fields belonging to the tomb, the firstfruits of the harvest

* One of the Egyptian festivals of the dead.

though the prince's domain, as each commoner in Siout is accustomed to do from the firstfruits of his harvest, for every peasant always makes a gift from the firstfruits of his harvest to the temple."* The ceremonial is set out in detail, and the monument tells us how, and under what conditions, a dead person is fed in Egypt. The loaves, meat and corn were placed in front of the statue by the priests: thence they reached the gods, who, after taking their part, transmitted the rest to the *double*.

We now understand why the statues that do not represent gods are always and uniquely portraits as exact as the artists could render them. Each was a stone body; not an ideal body in which only beauty of form or expression was sought, but a real body in which care should be taken neither to add nor take away anything. If the body of flesh had been ugly, the body of stone must be ugly in the same way, otherwise the *double* would not find the support it needed. The statue from which the head preserved in the Louvre was broken off was, undoubtedly, the faithful portrait of the individual whose name was engraved on it: if the realism of the expression is somewhat brutal, it is the fault of the model, who had not taken care to be handsome, and not that of the sculptor, who would have been guilty of a sort of impiety if he had altered the physiognomy of his model in the least detail.

* For complete translation of the contract see the *Transactions of the Society of Biblical Archæology*, vol. vii., pp. 1–9.

IV

SKHEMKA, HIS WIFE AND SON
A GROUP FOUND AT MEMPHIS

(*The Louvre*)

SKHEMKA lived at Memphis at the end of the Vth Dynasty. He was attached to the administration of the domains, and was buried in the necropolis of Saqqarah. His tomb, discovered by Mariette during the excavations of the Serapeum, furnished three pretty statues to the Louvre.* I knew the group reproduced here at a time when the coating that covered it had suffered very little; the galleries of Europe possess nothing to be compared with it for finish of execution.

I shall not say much of the principal personage: he possesses all the qualities and all the defects to which we are accustomed in the work of the sculptors of the Ancient Empire. The modelling of the torso, arms, and legs is excellent, of the foot mediocre, of the hands execrable; the head lives, alive and intelligent under the large wig, with its rows of braids one above the other,

---

* The Skhemka group was catalogued for the first time by E. de Rougé, "Notice sommaire des Monuments égyptiens," 1855, pp. 50–51, under the number S. 102. The other two statues of the same person possessed by the Museum are both entered under the number S.103. One is in granite, the other in painted limestone.

Studies in Egyptian Art

which frames it. The two accessory statues are charming in design and composition. On the left Ati, the dead man's wife, stands leaning against the back of the seat embracing her husband's leg. The face and limbs are painted yellow in accordance with a convention almost always respected in Egypt.* A layer of bright red denotes the tan that the sun lays on the men's skin; the light yellow reproduces the more delicate shade induced by the indoor life of the women. The hair, parted over the forehead, falls in two masses alongside the cheeks. The sleeveless dress is open in front, and the opening extends in a point to between the two breasts: the stuff exactly follows the lines of the body, and the skirt ends a little above the ankle. The position of the breasts is indicated by a special design; all the rest from the waist to the feet is embroidered with ornaments in colour, imitating the network of glass beads to be seen in the museums.† A necklace with two rows and bracelets complete the costume. On the right,, Knom, son of Skhemka and Ati, serves as a pendant to his mother: he is naked except for a necklace round the bottom of his neck and a little square amulet that falls on his chest. The grace and charm of the figures cannot be too much admired. Although of small dimensions, the artist has endowed them with the physiognomy and features suited to their age with as much exactness as if he had been dealing with a colossus. The firm flesh and rounded but

---

* There are exceptions only in the middle of the XVIIIth Dynasty, when men and women, and especially women, are painted light pink or flesh colour.

† The pretty painted bas-relief of the tomb of Seti I in the Louvre (E. de Rougé, " Notice des principaux monuments," p. 35, B. 7) shows in large the arrangement of the glass beads on the stuff.

SKHEMKA WITH HIS WIFE AND SON.
Limestone. The Louvre

Skhemka, His Wife and Son

muscular limbs of the woman in her prime, and the chubby flesh and soft limbs of the child, are treated equally happily. The mother's face has a smiling charm, the son's a naïve and wondering grace : the Egyptian chisel did not often work with so much intelligence and lightness.

The gesture with which each of the two small people embraces the leg of the big one is not an artifice of composition, a simple way of attaching the subordinate elements of the group to the principal one. It is often to be found in turning over the plates of Lepsius's fine work.* The inscriptions repeatedly state of the wife that "she loved her husband," and the artists reveal it in action. Seated or standing by his side, she puts her hand on his shoulder or her arm round his neck; crouching or kneeling, she leans against him, her breast pressed against his leg, her cheek leaning against his knee. And it is not only in the privacy of the home that she treats him with this affectionate abandon, but in public, before the servants or the assembled vassals, while he is inspecting his lands and reviewing his possessions.†

* Cf., e.g., Lepsius, "Denkmäler," ii., 47b, 74e, where the woman crouching in front of her husband puts her arm round his leg.

† Here are some references to plates in Lepsius where the husband and wife are represented side by side in different positions. The woman of low stature crouches behind her seated husband ("Denkmäler," ii., 71b); the wife and husband, both of heroic stature, are seated on the same armchair, and the wife puts her right arm round her husband's neck ("Denkmäler," ii., 10b, 24, 25b, 41b, 42a-b, 75a, etc.); the wife of low stature stands in front of her husband, who is of heroic stature ("Denkmäler," ii., 38b); she stands behind him and puts her arm round his left arm ("Denkmäler," ii., 27, 33a), or she puts her arm round his waist ("Denkmäler," ii., 38a); and lastly, the husband and wife, of the same stature, are standing, the wife behind her husband and putting her arm round his neck ("Denkmäler," ii., 13, 20-1, 29b, 32, 34b, 40b, 43b, 46, 58a, 59b), or separated from him ("Denkmäler," ii., 73, etc.).

Studies in Egyptian Art

In the same way it is rare to find a personage without his children, "who love him," at his feet or by his side, from the little, naked long-haired boy, like Knom, to the grown-up sons and married daughters. To sum up, the sculptor to whom we owe the Louvre monument has carved in stone a scene of contemporary life. He shows us Skhemka, Ati, and Knom grouped as they were every day: and what is conventional in his work is not the grouping of the three people, but the disproportion in stature between the husband and wife, and between the mother and son.

But here, again, he is only conforming to a prevailing tradition of his art. In all the tombs of every period, the master of the hypogeum is generally of the height of the wall, while servants, friends, sons, and wives are only of the height of one of the rows. The king, in the warlike paintings of the temples, is of colossal size, while the others, friends or enemies, beside him, look like a crowd of pigmies. In that case we might imagine that the difference in size showed only the difference of rank, but the explanation does not suffice elsewhere. A slave married for her beauty preserved something of the inferiority of her former condition; a princess of the blood royal, united in marriage to a private individual, did not therefore renounce her royal rank. If inequality of stature corresponded to inequality of rank, the sculptor would have made the first smaller and the second bigger than her husband. They did not, however, do that: slave or princess, they gave the wife a stature sometimes equal but more often lower than that of the husband.* Thus

* Thus in Lepsius ("Denkmäler," ii., 74e), where the noble Senotmhît, surnamed Mihi, is seated, of heroic stature, while his wife, Khontkaous, is represented crouching and of low stature,

Skhemka, His Wife and Son

the treatment does not show social distinction; the woman was legally on the same level as the man. If the master of the tomb is alone in his height, it is merely because he alone is at home in the tomb, and it was desired to show in him the one master, the personage who must be protected against the dangers of the other world: so he was designed of large size, as we underline a word in a sentence in order to emphasize it.

In fact, the sculptor, in modelling his work, thought of the necessities of the life beyond the tomb. Skhemka's wife living might be superior to Skhemka by fortune or birth, and so take precedence of him; before the dead Skhemka she was only a subordinate personage. Egyptian theology supposed, it would seem, that the wife was as indispensable to the man after as during life, and that is why she is represented by his side on the walls of his tomb; but, as she is only an accessory there, the sculptor and the painter are free to treat her as they understand the matter. If the husband demanded it, they gave both the same stature, seated them on the same seat, made no sort of difference between them. But if he expressed no wish, they could either suppress her altogether or relegate her to the background and give her the dimensions of her son, as they did with Ati, in order that she may lean against the seat on which her husband is enthroned.

although she is a legitimate daughter of the king. In another part of the tomb (Lepsius, "Denkmäler," ii., 73) the same persons are represented standing side by side and of heroic stature, while their children are of ordinary stature.

V

THE CROUCHING SCRIBE
Vth DYNASTY

(*The Louvre*)

HE was found by Mariette in the tomb of Skhemka in 1851, during the soundings which preceded the discovery of the Serapeum. He is now in the Louvre, in the centre of the "Salle civile" of the Egyptian Gallery, surrounded by show-case tables. His attitude, in conjunction with the unfortunate place assigned him, makes him look like a fellah dealer in antiquities seated in the midst of his goods, patiently waiting for customers. The red paint, which was perfect when he was brought to the Louvre, has worn off in places with the coating on which it was applied, and so the whity colour of the limestone shows through here and there; the cross light from the two windows falls on him in such a way as almost to efface the modelling of the shoulders and chest: ordinary visitors, for whom there is nothing to mark it, scarcely look at it, and pass it by in complete indifference to the fact that one of the masterpieces of Egyptian sculpture is before them.

Does he represent the great lord in whose tomb he was found? Other statues that entered the Louvre with his bear the name of Skhemka and pass for

CROUCHING SCRIBE.
The Louvre.

The Crouching Scribe

the faithful portrait of that personage.* If, as their careful composition leads us to believe, that claim is justified, the Crouching Scribe was only one of the numerous relatives or servants named in the inscriptions of the chapel. The people of the Ancient Empire had the custom of shutting up in the *Serdâb*,† by the side of the statue of the dead person, those of other individuals belonging to his family or his household. They are mourners, both men and women crouching down, one hand hanging or cast on the ground about to pick up the dust in sign of mourning, the other held in front of the face and plunged into the hair; ‡ women who crush the grain on the stone; servants who thrust their arm into an amphora, probably to coat it with pitch before pouring in the beer or wine. Ours is a scribe: his legs bent under him and placed flat on the ground in one of those positions familiar to Orientals, but almost impossible for Europeans, the bust upright and well-balanced on the hips, the head raised; reed in hand, and the sheet of papyrus spread over his knees, he still waits, at an interval of 6,000 years, for his master to resume the interrupted dictation. The paintings in the contemporary tombs tell us a hundred times rather than once what he is preparing to write. In order to sustain himself in the other world, the great Egyptian lord received on appointed days the offerings due to him from the domains attached to his tomb: one was to bring bread, one meat, others wine,

---

* See the preceding chapter, pp. 55–59.

† See Chapter III, p. 51.

‡ We know now (1912) that the figures described by Mariette as mourners are cooks, who held the spit in one hand and with the other protected their faces from the heat of the brazier where the chickens were roasting.

Studies in Egyptian Art

cakes, fruit. It was quite a big piece of bookkeeping, identical with that usual in his lifetime. The scribes of flesh and blood entered the real revenues as they came in; the scribe of stone rendered the same service to the master of stone whom he attended for ever.

We cannot say that our scribe was handsome in his lifetime, but the truth and vigour of his portrait compensates largely for what he lacks in beauty. The face is almost square, and the strongly accentuated features indicate a man in his prime; the large mouth with thin lips is slightly raised at the corners and almost disappears in the prominent muscles that frame it; the cheeks are rather hard and bony; the ears are thick and heavy, and stand out awkwardly from the head; and the low brow is crowned with coarse, short hair. The eye is well opened, and owes its special vivacity to an artifice of the ancient sculptor. The stone in which it is set has been cut away and the hollow filled with black and white enamel; a bronze mounting marks the edges of the eyelids, while a little silver nail* fastened under the crystal at the bottom of the eyeball receives the light, and reflecting it, simulates the pupil of a real eye. It is difficult to imagine the striking effect that this combination may produce in certain circumstances. When Mariette cleared out the tomb of Râhotpou at Meîdoum, the first ray of light which entered the tomb, that had been closed for 6,000 years, fell on the forehead of two statues leaning against the wall of the *Serdâb,* and made the eyes sparkle so brilliantly that the fellahs threw down their

---

* In examining the eye of the Cheikh-el-Beled closely, I found that there was no silver nail in it, but that the luminous spangle was produced by a scrap of polished ebony placed under the crystal; it should be the same with the eyes of the Crouching Scribe.

The Crouching Scribe

tools and fled in terror. Recovered from their fear, they wanted to destroy the statues, persuaded that they contained an evil genius, and were only prevented from doing so at the point of the pistol. More than one statue of the Ancient Empire, intact at the moment of its discovery, was mutilated for the same reason that nearly proved fatal to those of Meîdoum. In the bad light in which the Crouching Scribe is placed, the eyeball does not shine with a sufficiently strong sparkle, but it really does seem to have life in it and to follow the visitor with its look.

The rest of the body is equally full of expression. The flesh hangs a little, as is fitting with a man of a certain age whose occupations prevent exercise. The arms and back are good in detail; the lean bony hands have fingers of a greater length than is usual; the rendering of the knee is minute and exact in a way rarely found elsewhere in Egyptian art. The whole body is, so to speak, governed by the animation of the physiognomy, and under the influence of the same feeling of expectation that dominates it: the muscles of the arm, bust, and shoulder are only partly at rest, ready at the first signal to resume the task that has been begun. No work better refutes the reproach of stiffness usually made in regard to Egyptian art. Let us add that it is unique in Europe, and that we must go to Boulaq for pieces fine enough to sustain comparison without disadvantage. But it is not enough to possess a masterpiece, it is still more important to preserve it. In its present position the Crouching Scribe runs more risks than formerly in Egypt. The thousands of years spent buried beneath the sand in a hypogeum on the tableland of Saqqarah thoroughly dried up the limestone of which it is made.

Studies in Egyptian Art

Transported to our damp climate, and submitted to its sudden changes of temperature, it is only too much exposed to deterioration. It should not have been installed without protection and naked, so to say, in the centre of a room, between two large doors always open, round about which there are perpetual draughts. The curators at Turin have placed the fine limestone statue of Amenophis I possessed by the Museum in a tightly closed glass cage, and to that protection is due the fact that the Pharaoh has preserved its epidermis and colour intact; the expense is not so great that the Louvre would be impoverished by authorizing a similar proceeding. The demotic inscriptions of the Serapeum are carefully placed under glass, and the precaution is praiseworthy, although it makes the study of them impossible; it is then high time to take similar precautions with the Scribe. The damp has already acted on it a little; the red coating has been loosened and has fallen away in some places. If the mechanical work of destruction is allowed to proceed it will soon be in the same condition as the three statues of Sapoui and his wife, and the Louvre will have lost one of the finest pieces of sculpture Egypt has given us.

In comparing it with the statues of Skhemka that we have already described,* we are led to ask why the statue of a subordinate person should be so superior to that of his master. The Egyptians knew nothing of what we term art and the artist's profession: their sculptors were persons who cut stone with more or less skill, but whose work, always subordinated to the plan of a building, or to theological considerations, did not possess the absolute value belonging to the least impor-

* Cf. pp. 55–59.

The Crouching Scribe

tant statue of classical antiquity or of modern times. The effigy of an individual was placed in his tomb, not because it was beautiful, but because it represented him and served as a support to his *double*. The question of skill or artistic feeling was a subordinate one, and we find twenty statues of the same person, some of which are of finished workmanship and others coarse sketches: whether a masterpiece or not, the stone body equally served its purpose. Skhemka fell into the hands of a merely conscientious workman, his scribe into those of a highly skilled craftsman. I imagine that they cared little enough if the sculptor brought more or less talent to his task: so long as the resemblance was there, they asked for nothing more.

VI

THE NEW SCRIBE OF THE GIZEH MUSEUM*

THE excavations undertaken by M. de Morgan in the northern part of the necropolis of Saqqarah have recently brought to light a mastaba in fine white stone, near the tomb of Sabou, a little to the east of Mariette's old house. No architectural façade or chapels accessible to the living were found, only a narrow corridor that plunges into the masonry from north to south with 5° deviation to the east. The walls had been prepared and made smooth to receive the usual decoration, but when the mason had completed his task, the sculptor, it would seem, had no time to begin his. None of the sketches with the chisel or brush customarily found in the unfinished tombs of all periods are to be seen. Two large stelæ, or, if it is preferred, two niches in the form of doors, had been prepared in the right-hand wall, and a statue stood in front of each in the same spot where the Egyptian workmen had placed them on the day of the funeral. The first represents a man seated squarely on a stool, wearing the loin-cloth, and on his head a wig with rows of small curls one above the other.

---

* This article was published in two slightly different forms in the *Gazette des Beaux-Arts*, 3rd period, 1893, vol. ix., pp. 265-70, and in the *Monuments Piot*, 1894, vol. i., pp. 1-6 : I have combined them for this volume.

THE NEW SCRIBE OF THE GIZEH MUSEUM.
Painted limestone.

Scribe of the Gizeh Museum

The bust and legs are bare; the fore-arms and hands rest on the knees, the right hand closed with the thumb sticking out, the left flat with the tips of the fingers reaching beyond the hem of the loin-cloth. So far as may be judged from a photograph, the general style is somewhat weak; but the detail of the knee, the structure of the leg and foot, are carefully rendered, the chest and back stand out by the excellent modelling, the head, weighted as it is by the coiffure, is attached to the shoulder with an easy and not ungraceful vivacity. The face is not in good relief, and has a sheepish expression, but the mouth is smiling, and the eyes of quartz and crystal have an extraordinarily gentle expression. Taken altogether it is a very good piece of Egyptian portraiture, and would be a valuable addition to any museum.*

The new scribe was crouching in front of the second stele.† He measures in height almost the same as his colleague in the Louvre, and sufficiently resembles him to permit both being described in almost similar terms. The legs are bent under and are flat on the ground, the bust upright and well balanced on the hips, the head raised, the hand armed with the reed, and in its place on the open papyrus sheet; they are both waiting at an interval of 6,000 years for the master to resume the interrupted dictation.‡ The professional gesture and attitude are reproduced with a truth that leaves nothing to be desired: it is not only a scribe whom we have before us, it is the scribe as the Egyptians knew him from the beginning of their history. The skill with which

---

* The statue is described in the "Visitor's Guide to the Cairo Museum," 2nd edition, 1912, p. 58, No. 142.

† Maspero, "Visitor's Guide," 2nd edition, 1912, pp. 57-8, No. 141.

‡ Cf. p. 61.

Studies in Egyptian Art

the sculptors have brought out and co-ordinated the general features belonging to each class of society is largely responsible for the impression of monotony produced by their works on modern spectators. That impression is lessened and nearly effaced, if we look a little more closely and see how carefully the sculptors have noted and reproduced the details of form and bearing that make up the physiognomy proper to each of the individuals who live in the same social surroundings or practise the same profession. Our two scribes do not cross their legs in identical fashion; he of the Louvre puts the right leg in front, he of Gizeh the left. There is no fixed choice, and children at first tuck their legs under without thought of preference for one or the other; soon they acquire a habit which makes them keep to the position once adopted, and in the East to-day you find people who put either the left or right leg in front, and just a few who put either one or the other indifferently. The Louvre scribe flattens out the hand that holds the reed, the man of Gizeh sinks down, and his back is slightly bent. This shows the habit of the individual, and is not a question of age, for a glance at the two statues shows that the Gizeh scribe is younger than his colleague of the Louvre: he is not out of the thirties, while the other is certainly over forty.

Indeed, the age of the two men is an important point of which we must not lose sight, if we desire to judge soberly the real value of the two works. I have heard archæologists, when comparing them, regret that the scribe of Gizeh does not show the same abundance of carefully studied anatomical detail as the scribe of the Louvre; that therein lies the real inferiority of the first, whether it was that the sculptor was less conversant with

Scribe of the Gizeh Museum

the anatomy of the human body than with that of the face, or that time had pressed, and he had contented himself with giving his subject the conventional body that for the most part sufficed in funerary statues. The care, as I have pointed out, with which the small details of the attitude are expressed shows that the reproach is undeserved, and that the artist has worked to give a portrait complete from top to toe, and not only to reproduce a head on a conventional body. The roundness of the form preserves the appearance of the original, and shows, realistically, the age the subject was at the time of his death, or at least at the period of life at which his relatives desired to have a portrait of him. In the best facsimile something of the delicacy of the monument itself must be lost, and in spite of the great care taken in engraving it, its original aspect is not entirely preserved. I think, however, that in looking closely at it there can still be seen in many places the artistic, supple workmanship by which the chisel expressed the delicacy and vigour of the model. The most vigorous fellah of our day, when young and in good health, has apparently slender muscles that do not stand out: like those of the porters of Boulaq, one of whom without aid moved a stone statue of nearly the same height as himself, and yet had hands and calves like those of a woman, that looked of slight strength and incapable of continuous effort. The knotty and twisted excrescences to be seen on the arms, back, or chest of our athletes were rarely found in Egyptians of ancient race, at least in youth. The ancient sculptor rightly noted that physiological trait of his people. He had a young man before him: so he evolved from the limestone a young Egyptian body in which the play of the muscles is hidden beneath the skin, and is only betrayed by a number of touches manipulated with knowledge and discretion. If, like his colleague who sculptured the Louvre scribe, he had had to portray a person of ripe age, he would not have exerted himself to bring out the flabbiness of the flesh and the heaviness of its folds, to execute all the pleasant work of the chisel which so well reproduces the depredations of age in a rich sedentary man of fifty. In short, he worked differently because he had a different subject.

There is no sort of inscription on either statue to inform us of the name and characteristics of its original, who must have been a person of some importance: a large tomb invariably meant a considerable fortune, or a high post in the administrative hierarchy which compensated for mediocrity of fortune. It might also be that Pharaoh, desiring to reward services rendered him by some one in his *entourage*, granted him a statue, a stele, an entire tomb built by the royal architects at the expense of the Treasury.* It is certain that our anonymous scribe held high rank in his lifetime, but to what Dynasty did he belong? He so closely resembles the scribe of the Louvre that he was evidently his contemporary: he must then have lived at the end of the Vth Dynasty, and we reach a similar result if we compare him with the other statues preserved at Gizeh. It is of the style of the statues of Ti and of Rânofir, especially of the last two. One of them, which formerly was No. 975 in the Boulaq Museum, is full of dignified feeling.† Rânofir is standing, his two arms pressed against his

---

* Cf. what has already been said regarding statues of private individuals erected by the favour of the Pharaoh, p. 40.

† Maspero, "Visitor's Guide to the Boulaq Museum," p. 28, and now "Visitor's Guide to the Cairo Museum," 2nd edition, 1912, p. 73, No. 227.

Scribe of the Gizeh Museum

body, one leg in advance, in the attitude of a prince who is looking at his vassals march past him. Whoever has seen him cannot fail to observe how much he resembles our new scribe. Firstly, the head-dress is the same; they both have the head framed, so to speak, in a bell-mouthed wig. The hairs or fibres of which it is made were gummed, as is the case to-day with the hair of certain African tribes. The hair is carefully smoothed on the forehead and the top of the head, and being parted on the cranium, hangs down and forms a kind of dark case round the face which accentuates the ruddy tint of the flesh. The modelling of the torso, the muscling of the arms, are treated in the same way in both statues, and the dignified expression which characterizes the physiognomy of Rânofir relieves the somewhat commonplace features of the new scribe. Those are all facts that are not to be noted in other portraits of our personages. The seated statue that I first described possesses the general aspect of the individual, and undoubtedly represents him; but the technique and feeling differ, since it is necessarily that of a different sculptor. It is the same with Rânofir. The statue of him numbered 1049 in the Boulaq Museum lacks the high dignity we admire in No. 975. It is so heavy, so expressionless, that it almost seems to be another Egyptian. The difference in the workmanship proves that two artists were commissioned to execute statues of the same man. The identity of workmanship, on the other hand, compels us to recognize the same hand in the statue No. 975 of Rânofir and in that of our new scribe: the two works proceeded almost at the same time from one studio.

It would be interesting to find out if, among the statues in the museums, there are others that may be related to these

Studies in Egyptian Art

and have a common origin. I do not so far know any, but I ought to add to what I have said the indication of a special sign by which they can be distinguished. The Egyptians were accustomed to paint their statues and basreliefs, and the colours in which they clothed them were more varied, and more subject to change, than is generally recognized. We are used to see only a red-brown tone for the flesh, and they certainly employed it very often; they did not, however, employ that tone only, and men's faces are occasionally coloured in a very different way. The colouring of statue No. 975 and of the new scribe differs from the usual manner. That of statue No. 975 has grown paler since Rânofir left his tomb and became exposed to the light, but that of the Gizeh scribe is still fresh, and resembles as faithfully as possible the yellow complexion bordering on red of the modern fellah. The greater number of archæologists who occupy themselves with Egyptian art neglect facts of this kind. During my stay in Egypt I have endeavoured to bring them out, and it is in co-ordinating them systematically that I have been able to verify the existence, either at Memphis itself or in the ancient village of Saqqarah, of two principal studios of

STATUE OF RÂNOFIR.
Cairo Museum.

Scribe of the Gizeh Museum

sculptors and painters to which customers of the later periods of the Vth Dynasty entrusted the task of decorating the tombs and carving the funerary statues.

Each had its special style, its traditions, its models, from which it did not willingly depart. Commissions were divided between them in unequal proportions, according to whether it was a question of isolated statues or of bas-reliefs. I do not remember observing sensible differences of style in the pictures that cover the walls of the same mastaba: for that kind of work application was made to one or the other studio, and it alone undertook the commission. For the statues, on the contrary, recourse was had to both at the same time: the task, thus divided, was more quickly accomplished, and there was more chance that it would be finished by the day of the funeral. I do not mean to state that there were then only the two studios of which I speak: I think I have found traces of several others, but they perhaps enjoyed less vogue, or the chances of excavation have not so far been favourable to them.

To sum up, we may say, without the risk of being taxed with exaggeration, that the art of the Ancient Empire counts another masterpiece. It was a gift of happy chance to M. de Morgan in his first serious excavations as earnest of good fortune: it is of good augury for the future, and, as he is not a man to let a chance slip once he holds it, and since he has the material means and the money required for methodical exploration, we may hope for further finds without long delay.

VII

THE KNEELING SCRIBE
V<small>TH</small> DYNASTY

(*Boulaq Museum*)

I<small>F</small> he had not been dead for 6,000 years, I should swear that I met him six months ago in a little town of Upper Egypt. It was the same commonplace round face, the same flattened nose, the same full mouth, slightly contracted on the left by a foolish smile, the same banal expressionless physiognomy: the costume alone was different and prevented the illusion from being complete. The loin-cloth is no longer in fashion, and neither is the large wig; except the fellahs when at work, no one now goes about with bare legs and torso. Some follow fairly closely the custom of Cairo, and wear the too small tarbouche, the stiff stambouline, the European starched shirt, but without a cravat, black or crude blue trousers, shoes with cloth gaiters. Others keep to the turban, long gown, wide trousers, and red or yellow morocco leather babouches. But if his clothes have changed since the Vth Dynasty, his deportment has remained perceivably identical. The modern secretary, after delivering his papers to his master, crosses his hands over his chest or his stomach in the fashion of the ancient scribe; he no longer kneels while waiting, but assumes the humblest attitude imaginable, and if his costume did not

KNEELING SCRIBE.
Cairo Museum.

The Kneeling Scribe

hide it, we should recognize the suppleness that characterizes the Boulaq statue in the movement of his shoulders and spine. His chief finishes reading the papers, affixes his seal to this one or that, writes a few lines across another, and throws the sheets on the ground: the secretary picks them up, and returns to his office without offence at the cavalier manner in which his work is given back to him. Indeed, is it to be expected that a moudir, a man receiving a large salary, would take the trouble to stretch out his arm to meet the hand of a mere ill-paid employee? In fact, he treats his subordinates as his superiors treat him; his subordinates, in their turn, act in a similar way towards theirs, and so things go on right down the ladder, and no one dreams of objecting.

Our scribe was one of those to whom the papers were thrown more often than to others. He occupied a somewhat low place in the hierarchy, and no bond attached him to the great families of his period. If he is kneeling, it is that the sculptor has represented him in one of his ordinary attitudes during the hours of work; he has also drawn his portrait with the fidelity and jovial good humour adopted by artists in portraying scenes of everyday life. The man has just brought a roll of papyrus or a tray laden with papers; kneeling in the approved manner, the bust well-balanced on the hips, the hands crossed, the back bowed, the head slightly bent, he waits until his master has finished reading. Does he think? Scribes felt some secret apprehension when appearing before their masters. The rod played a large part in the discipline of the offices. An error in the addition of an account, a word omitted in copying a letter, an instruction misunderstood, an order awkwardly executed, and the blows fell. Few employees escaped flogging. If they did not deserve it, it would be

Studies in Egyptian Art

inflicted on principle: "That young fellow requires a beating. He obeys when he is flogged !"* The sculptor has admirably transferred to the stone the expression of resigned uncertainty and sheepish gentleness with which the routine of an entire life spent in service had endowed the model. The mouth is smiling, for such is the demand of etiquette, but there is no joy in the smile. The nose and cheeks grimace in unison with the mouth. The two big enamel eyes, surrounded with bronze, have the fixed expression of a man who is vaguely waiting, without looking attentively at anything or concentrating his thought on a definite object. The face lacks intelligence and vivacity. After all, the profession did not exact great alertness of mind. The formulas of administration were simple and of little variety, the arithmetic was not complicated; it was possible to get on easily with memory and industry, and so, without much trouble, to earn sufficient to purchase a good funerary statue.

Our statue was found at Saqqarah † in a tomb of somewhat mediocre appearance. Neither the name nor

* The expression is borrowed from a letter of the *Papyrus Anastasis*, No. 3. Its position in the Egyptian context leads me to believe that it was an often-quoted proverb. The idea is repeated in different forms in the scribes' correspondence: "Work, or you will be beaten." "When the scribe reaches the age of manhood, his back is broken by the blows he has received."

† Mariette, "Notice des principaux monuments du Musée de Boulaq," 6th edition, 1876, p. 235, No. 769 : " Memphis. Saqqarah— limestone II, 1 foot 2 inches—kneeling figure. His hands crossed on his legs. His eyes are of mosaic work and formed of several stones curiously combined." The statue of the kneeling scribe figures in a group in Plate XX of Mariette's work, "Album du Musée de Boulaq," containing 40 plates, photographed by MM. Délié and Béchard, with explanatory text edited by Auguste Mariette-Bey. Cairo, Mourès et Cie, 1871, fol.

The Kneeling Scribe

filiation of the man informs us under what king or Dynasty he vegetated; but in comparing him with the statue of Rânofir * we are able to assign him his place in the series. First, both our scribe and Rânofir wear a wig of a form somewhat rare at that period; the hair, parted from the centre of the brow, is drawn back in a mass behind the ears and hangs down straight round the neck. Our scribe, instead of the red complexion usually attributed to men's faces, is painted light yellow, very like those of women. Rânofir shows the same peculiarity, an unusual one under the Ancient Empire. I do not think it could have been mere caprice on the part of the artist. A scribe, forced to live always in his office as women do in their homes, would have a less sunburnt skin than his colleagues who worked in the open air: the yellow colour of the limestone would thus be a sort of professional sign, and would correspond with a lighter complexion in the original. The titles of Rânofir prove that he lived under the last reigns of the Vth Dynasty,† and in placing the kneeling scribe at the same period, we are sure of not being much in error. I have preferred to base my opinions on purely archæological grounds, but I think an examination of the style of the two statues would carry the connection still farther: the

---

* Mariette, "Notice des principaux monuments du Musée de Boulaq," 6th edition, 1876, p. 216, No. 582. The Boulaq Museum possesses a second statue of the same person (*ibid.*, p. 93, No. 28), but of a less fine execution than the statue No. 582. Cf. what is said of the two statues on pp. 70–73 of this volume.

† Mariette, "Notice," p. 217: "The sum of the qualities, and study of the inscriptions on the base of the monument, leave no doubt as to the epoch to which it belongs. Rânofir evidently lived under the Ancient Empire. His titles bring him near the Vth Dynasty." The study of the inscriptions leads me to be more certain than Mariette was. Rânofir undoubtedly lived at the end of the Vth Dynasty.

Studies in Egyptian Art

way in which the neck is attached to the shoulders, and particularly the way in which the hands are treated, is almost identical in the two cases. I do not know if I am mistaken, but I have almost persuaded myself that the statue of Rânofir and that of the kneeling scribe come from the same studio, and are perhaps the fruit of the same chisel. I do not despair of finding other monuments of a similar origin, and of reconstituting in part the work of one of the masters of which the tombs of Memphis have preserved the various productions, but without preserving their names.

The execution is very careful: unfortunately the limestone in which the scribe is cut was too soft, and it is worn away in places. The knees have suffered most, and it is a great pity, for we can see by what is left of them how careful the artist has been with the modelling. The arms are not divided from the bust, the hands are heavy, the feet long, but the play of the muscles of the chest and neck is well noted. In short, it is an estimable work of a conscientious sculptor who thoroughly understood his vocation.

VIII

PEHOURNOWRI
STATUETTE IN PAINTED LIMESTONE FOUND AT MEMPHIS

(*The Louvre*)

MARIETTE found the statuette by chance when searching the Serapeum. It had formerly been taken from the pit in which it was shut up and thrown amid the rubbish of the great sphinx avenue that leads to the tomb of Apis. The individual was named Pehournowri; he was cousin royal, and fulfilled functions that I do not know how to define. Nothing in the inscription helps us to conjecture with what king he claimed relationship, but its style proves that he lived under the Vth Dynasty. That he was of mature age is indicated by the plenitude of form, by the fine proportions and the benevolent and benign aspect. A short wig, a necklace, a loin-cloth scarcely reaching the knees, completes his costume. His statue is not one in front of which we naturally pause when walking through a museum. I do not think that during the thirty years it has been in the Louvre it has attracted the attention of any one except experts in Egyptology. Not that it lacks merit: the modelling is exact, the execution skilful and delicate, the expression frank and successful, but the pose differs very slightly from that which hundreds of other artists have given to hundreds

Studies in Egyptian Art

of other statues. The careless visitor who passes from one seated man to a second, and then to many others, does not think of looking for the details of execution that distinguish them. He thinks that when he has seen one or two he has seen all, and departs with the idea that the chief attribute of Egyptian art is monotony.

Egyptian sculptors did not greatly vary the pose of their sitters. Sometimes they represented them standing and walking, one leg in advance of the other, sometimes standing, but motionless, with the feet together, sometimes sitting on a seat or a stone pedestal, sometimes kneeling, more often crouching, the chin against the knees like the fellahs of to-day, or the legs flat on the ground like the scribe of the Louvre.* The details of arrangement and costume may be modified *ad infinitum*, but the attitude is nearly always regulated by the six types I have enumerated. Some modern critics attribute this fact to the inexperience of the sculptors, others to the inflexibility of certain hieratical rules. But having seen not only the few incomplete pieces to be found in Europe, but also the monuments still existing in Egypt, I cannot admit those reasons. Everywhere in the bas-reliefs of the temples and tombs a multiplicity of gestures or attitudes are to be seen which show to what point the artists could, when they pleased, diversify the human figure: the peasant bends over the hoe, the joiner leans over his bench, the scribe stoops over his paper, the dancers, girls and men, twist and balance their bodies, the soldiers brandish their lances or march in time, as naturally as possible. And the sculptors even reproduced positions in their statues very different from those we are accustomed to see at the Louvre: the kneeling woman who is grind-

* See pp. 60–65.

PEHOURNOWRI
The Louvre.

Pehournowri Statuette

ing her corn, the baker who is kneading the dough, the slave who coats the amphora with pitch before pouring in the wine, the crouching mourner of Boulaq,* are all composed and modelled with a lightness of action and a perfection of expression that leaves no doubt as to the skill of the artist. It is true that hieratical rules existed, and no one will dispute that fact, but they were reserved for matters of religion and for those alone. They exacted, for instance, that Amon must always, in every case, have the attributes, costume, and attitude proper to the god, but they in no wise ordered that all men were to be confined to one of the five attitudes I have just described. The freedom of composition to which the large historical pictures of the temples or the domestic scenes of the tombs testify, does not agree with what we are told concerning the inflexibility of the hieratical rules.

I shall not now touch on the statues of kings or divinities: I shall have an opportunity later of treating them at leisure. Those of private individuals represent for the most part persons of rank, great nobles, people of the court, officers, magistrates, priests, employees of birth or fortune; they come from nearly all the cemeteries, and are portraits of the man for whom the tomb was hollowed out or of people of his house. The master stands in an attitude of command, or sits like Pehournowri, and he could only have one or the other of those attitudes. The tomb is, in fact, his private house, where he rests from the fatigues of life, as he used to do in his terrestrial home. A soldier when at home does not carry his arms, a magistrate does not wear his robe: soldier or magistrate, the insignia of the profession are laid aside when he returns home. Thus the master of

* He is a cook, as I mentioned on p. 61, note ‡.

Studies in Egyptian Art

the tomb always wears his civil costume, and leaves the marks of his profession at the door.

Then, also, the accessible part of his dwelling has a special destination which regulates the pose of the statues: it is, in fact, his reception-room, where on certain days the family assembled to present the offerings to him, in more prosaic words, to dine with him. Whether his statue was visible in one of the open chambers or invisible in the *Serdâb*,* it was his substitute. It is sufficient to look at the neighbouring bas-reliefs to discover what were the official attitudes of the dead man in the tomb. He was present at the preliminaries of the sacrifice, the sowing and the harvest, the rearing of the cattle, fishing, hunting, the execution of crafts, and he saw all the works carried out for the *eternal dwelling*: he was then standing, one foot in advance, head erect, hands hanging down, or armed with the staff of command. Elsewhere, one after the other, the different courses of the meal are served him, cakes, wines, canonical meats, fruits which he needs in the world of the dead: then he is seated in an armchair alone or with his wife. The sculptor employed for his statues the two positions he has in the paintings: standing, he receives the homage of his vassals; seated, he takes part in the meal. And in the same way the statues which embody the members of the family and of the household have likewise the attitude suited to their rank and occupation. The wife is sometimes standing, sometimes sitting on the same seat as her husband, or on a separate one; sometimes, as in life, crouching at his feet. The son wears the costume of childhood, if the statue was carved while he was still a child, or the costume and attitude of his office if he was an adult. The acting

* See p. 51.

Pehournowri Statuette

scribe crouches, the roll spread on his knees, as if he was writing from dictation or reading from an account-book.* The slave grinds the corn, the bakers knead the dough, the cellarers pitch their amphoras, the mourners lament and tear their hair as it was their duty to do in the world above; each individual is occupied according to his condition. The social hierarchy followed the Egyptian after death, and it regulated the pose of the statue after, as it had regulated that of the model before, death. Up to a certain point it is the same to-day, and he who carves the statue of a printer is careful not to attribute to him the action and costume of a miner or a sailor. These statues, shut up in the tomb, formed a sort of tableau in which each person held for ever the pose characteristic of his rank or his profession. The artist was free to vary the detail and regulate the accessories according to his fancy, but he could not change the general disposition without injuring the utility of his work.

At bottom, it is with the statues of Ancient Egypt as with the pictures of saints of the Italian schools. The painters had to treat their subject on lines from which they could not depart without falsifying or disfiguring it. Bring sixty or eighty St. Sebastians together in a room: how many of those who saw them would escape the boredom that infallibly results from constant repetition? When the tenth St. Sebastian was reached only a few professional artists would not have already gone away. I am supposing, too, that only choice pictures had been collected in which the qualities of a master are easily recognized. If, on the contrary, there had been collected at random all the available St. Sebastians without first eliminating the bad pictures, the finest St. Sebastians in

* See p. 61.

Studies in Egyptian Art

the world, lost in the crowd, would be likely to attract no more attention from the public than the Crouching Scribe or the other masterpieces of Egyptian sculpture in the Louvre. The hypothesis appears absurd, because no one will easily admit that any one could have the idea of making such a collection. I agree so far as modern or ancient works, the value of which is known, are concerned; but Egyptian Museums have so far always been classified as depôts of archæological objects, not as art galleries. Each statue is a scribe, a god, a king; it is the scribe Hor of the XIXth Dynasty, or the scribe Skhemka of the Vth, or the king Sovkhotpou, wearing the headdress of the pschent, and that is all. The trumpery scribes and the scribes that emanate from the hands of a master are confused under the same rubric, and no mark is placed to distinguish the good from the bad. Pehournowri is a scribe, Ramke a second scribe, Rahotpou a third scribe, just as the St. Sebastian of such or such a great Italian master and the St. Sebastians of the Epinal pictures are two St. Sebastians: the public which is not warned, and which has no more interest in one scribe than in another, passes on without looking.

The impression of monotony is produced by the perpetual repetition of the same types and by the method of classification adopted in the museums. If it was decided to do for Egypt what has been done for Greece and Rome, to separate the productions of art and the objects of archæology, people's opinion would be promptly modified. The impression of monotony would not wholly disappear, because the number of types studied by the Egyptian sculptors was not sufficiently numerous: it would be lessened and would no longer blind the crowd to the real beauty and perfection that reside in Egyptian sculpture.

IX

THE DWARF KHNOUMHOTPOU
(Vth OR VIth DYNASTY)

(*Boulaq Museum*)

THE charming person who left us this statue is known, since the Exhibition of 1878, by the name of the Superintendent of the Cooks; his title in the inscription on the pedestal indicates a keeper of the wardrobe. In his lifetime he doubtless enjoyed some notoriety, since he had one of the fine tombs of Saqqarah for himself alone, but we know nothing of his history. His name was Khnoumhotpou, a name later made illustrious by a prince of Minieh under the XIIth Dynasty: his place of burial proves that he was born at the end of the Vth or beginning of the VIth Dynasty.

He was a dwarf, and a very small dwarf. The statue is scarcely a foot in height, and the dimensions of the head show that it was probably half the natural size. It reproduces the characteristics proper to dwarfs without exaggerating them. The head, of a suitable size, is long-shaped and flanked by two large ears. The expression of the face is heavy and stupid, the eyes narrow and raised at the temples, and the mouth wide and ill-formed. The chest is strong and well developed, but the artist has employed his ingenuity in vain in order to dissimulate

Studies in Egyptian Art

the hind-quarters by covering them with a vast white petticoat; notwithstanding, we feel that the torso is not in proportion to the arms and legs. The stomach forms a round projection, and the hips recede in order to counterbalance the stomach. The thighs only exist in a rudimentary state, and the whole individual, mounted as he is on little deformed feet, seems about to fall face downwards on the ground. The flesh was painted red, the hair black, but the colour has peeled off or been effaced in places. The two legs were broken formerly at the ankle, then stuck on again when the statue was transported to the Museum. It is very possible that the accident happened during the execution of the statue, for the limestone used by the Egyptians is so fragile that the sculptor did not venture to detach the arms from the body: too hard a blow of the mallet while freeing the legs may have caused the unfortunate fracture that spoils the bottom of the monument.

Khnoumhotpou is, so far, the only dwarf that has come to light who is a nobleman. Similar dwarfs were not lacking in Egypt, but they nearly all belonged to the class of jugglers and buffoons. The Pharaohs and the princes of their court bestowed the same affection on these deformed creatures as did Christian or Mussulman kings in mediæval times; their household would not have been complete without two or three of them of an aspect more or less grotesque. Ti possessed one that figures by her in her tomb: the poor wretch holds in his right hand a kind of large wooden sceptre terminated by a model of a human hand, and leads a greyhound almost as tall as himself in a leash. Elsewhere dwarfs are represented crouching on a stool at the feet of their masters, by the side of the favourite monkey or dog. We know from

THE DWARF KHNOUMHOTPOU.
Cairo Museum.

The Dwarf Khnoumhotpou

the pictures of Beni-Hassan that two of them belonged to the prince of Minieh's suite; one, despite his small size, does not lack elegance, but the other enjoys with the exiguity of his stature the pleasure of being club-footed. The Egyptian heaven did not escape the prevailing mania any more than the court of the Pharaohs, and it included several dwarfs, of whom two at least had an important rôle : Bisa, who presided over arms and the toilet, and the Phtah, who for a long while has, without reason, been called embryonic Phtah.* Perhaps Knoumhotpou joined to his functions of keeper of the wardrobe the office of court buffoon; perhaps he was of noble birth, and preserved by his origin from the disagreeables to which his brethren of low extraction were exposed.

But we have no need to know what he was: merely in leaving us his portrait, he has rendered signal service to science. Let us recall the part played by the statues of the tombs in the theological conceptions of the Egyptians: they were the indispensable support of the *double*, the body without which the soul of the dead person could not exist in the other world. It might be thought that in passing from life in this world to that beyond the tomb, the people to whom beauty had been chary might not have been sorry to assume a new appearance; if we are to be re-born, it is better to be re-born less ugly. The care that poor Khnoumhotpou has taken to reach us deformed shows that the old Egyptians did not hold our views on the subject: they desired to remain always as nature created them at the

---

* See the curious study of Dr. Parrot, " Sur l'origine d'une des formes du dieu Phtah," in the " Recueil de travaux relatifs à la philologie et à l'archéologie égyptiennes et assyriennes," vol. ii., pp. 129-33.

Studies in Egyptian Art

moment of conception. It was not absence of coquetry on their part, but necessity: their idea of the soul compelled them so to act. From the moment that their personality was indissolubly bound up with the existence of the body, the first condition imposed on them for remaining identical with themselves after death, as before, was to preserve their earthly form intact. In order that the Khnoumhotpou who dwelt in the hypogeum of Saqqarah might not be a different being from the Khnoumhotpou who walked through the streets of Memphis, it was necessary that his disincarnated *double* should find there the support of a statue of a dwarf. Give him the fine proportions of Ti or Rânofir, the proud bearing and haughty mien of the Cheikh-el-Beled, even the more common type of the Crouching Scribe, he would not have known what to do. His substance, poured, so to speak, into the exiguous and deformed mould of the dwarf, could never have adapted itself to the new mould into which the artist would have tried to cast it. Khnoumhotpou beautified would no longer have been Khnoumhotpou; his tomb, without the statue of a dwarf, would only have sheltered a double and a support strangers to each other.

It was then the likeness, and the absolute likeness, that the artist had to seek to reproduce, and the seriousness and scrupulousness with which he rendered the deformity of his model is thus explained. The Egyptians were scoffers by nature, and liked to mingle the comic with the serious, not only in literature but in the arts. To take only one example: the painter who, at Thebes, pictured the interment of Nofrihotpou, has drawn, by the side of the large boats laden with mourners and all the apparatus of grief, the contortions of two sailors whose shallop

The Dwarf Khnoumhotpou

was brutally struck by the oars of the funerary barque. If the sculptor who chiselled Khnoumhotpou had been free to follow his natural inclination, he would probably have exaggerated certain features and given the unfortunate creature a slightly absurd physiognomy. His religious conscience would not permit him to risk anything of the kind: a statue uglier than nature would have been as inconvenient to the soul of the original as a statue more beautiful than nature. A body of stone identical at all points with the body of flesh was what the Egyptian demanded, and that is exactly what the sculptor fashioned for the little Khnoumhotpou. We see here that what we call the question of art is subsidiary: a stone-cutter who understood his business sufficed for all that was required.

It must not, however, be concluded from what precedes that I regard the portrait of Khnoumhotpou as the work of a mere artisan. It has been too often repeated that statuary in Egypt was a mechanical craft; sculptors were taught to fashion arms, legs, heads, and torsos, and to join them, according to the formula, in imitation of two or three models always the same. That opinion, repeated by the Greeks, is fairly difficult to uphold in the presence of the statue of Knoumhotpou; it might be possible to set up patterns for bodies of ordinary formation, but all varieties of deformed bodies could not possibly be foreseen. The unknown master whose work we have at Boulaq proceeded in exactly the same manner as a modern sculptor, the necessities of whose work confronted him with a deformed model: he produced a work of art, not the task of a mechanic.

X

THE FAVISSA OF KARNAK AND THE THEBAN SCHOOL OF SCULPTURE *

I

A LARGE pool among the ruins, and at the southern end two batteries of *chadoufs*, one on top of the other, working to exhaust the water continually renewed by the infiltrations. On the banks are blocks and muddy statues, round which half-naked workmen are busily occupied, beams, levers, coils of rope, and the beginnings of a Decauville line; remains of storied walls dominate the workshops, and the modern village of Karnak stands out clearly on the horizon beyond their irregular tops.

When the first Ptolemies decided at the beginning of the third century B.C. to restore the Theban temple of Amon, they found it encumbered with *ex-votos*. Everywhere, in the halls, the corridors, the court-yards, there were stelæ, stone statues, little wooden or bronze figures, sacred or royal insignia, heaped up one on the other, and in such quantities that there was no space for new ones. It was a legacy of extinct Dynasties or of noble families who had died out, to whom the Pharaohs had granted the privilege of consecrating their image in the house of the

* Published in the *Revue de l'Art ancien et moderne*, 1906, vol. xx., pp. 247–52, 337–48.

The Theban School of Sculpture

god, and to sell or destroy any of them would have been to commit sacrilege.* They were dealt with according to the custom of the contemporary peoples : a vast pit was dug between the seventh pylon and the hypostyle hall, and then they were buried pell-mell in holy ground. Twenty centuries later, in 1883, hastily made soundings revealed the richness of the site to me, but, lacking money, I could not venture to undertake anything. It was not until 1901, when the regular progress of clearing away brought the workmen to the spot, that I advised M. Legrain to dig more deeply than usual, so that nothing which was hidden beneath the earth might escape observation. The excavations yielded just what I had foreseen, royal colossi in granite, limestone, sandstone which were restored to their ancient places along the pylon ; a little below came fragments of a fine limestone building of Amenôthes I that Thoutmôsis III had used for banking up when he enlarged the temple ; and at the very bottom, at a depth of over six, twelve, fourteen yards, what none of us had thought of, an intact *favissa* in which hundreds of statues and small objects awaited in the mud the hour of their deliverance.

For four years M. Legrain has been exploring the spot foot by foot, and I think he has succeeded in entirely emptying it. We must now draw up the inventory of the treasures it has bestowed on us. The greatest benefit conferred by them is assuredly on political history. All epochs are not represented in equal abundance—the first Theban Empire is, so to speak, merely mentioned, and the two great Dynasties of the second are represented only by about a hundred pieces—but from the fall of the Ramessides to the Persian conquest the series of the high priests

* See pp. 50-51.

Studies in Egyptian Art

of Amon reappears almost complete, with their wives, sons, brothers, the children or latest descendants of their brothers, and from the day when the male line failed, the princesses who inherited its rights, with the noble persons who wielded the power in their name. However, the large find all at once of statues and inscriptions serves not only to give information about the revolution that transformed the military kingdom of Thebes into a theocracy, but also furnishes documents for the study of the progress of art during the twenty centuries and more that the revolution took. The artistic merit of the objects is very unequal, and many of them are only interesting to the archæologist; some, however, stand out distinguished above the mass, and take their rank worthily beside the best known productions of Egyptian art. As they come from the same temple, and have been erected by different members of the same families, it is natural to see in them the work of one school, established at Thebes in far-off antiquity. Indeed, a unity of character common to all is easily discerned, which, perpetuating itself without notable change from generation to generation, fixes undeniable affinities of conception and technique.

II

Setting aside a few stelæ in which the arrangement is bad and the composition coarse,* the most ancient monuments we possess of that school are those discovered by Carter and Naville between 1900 and 1906 in the tomb of Montouhotpou V at Deir-el-Bahari. The bas-reliefs of the chapel belonging to the pyramid are as correct in design

---

* See, *e.g.*, the stelæ described or referred to in Maspero, "Guide to the Cairo Museum," 1903, pp. 73–5, 94–5, 96, etc.

THE WORKS AT KARNAK IN JANUARY, 1906.

The Theban School of Sculpture

and as firm in touch as the fine Memphian bas-reliefs of the Vth or VIth Dynasty; but the relief is more accentuated, the outline bolder and freer, the man more thick-set, and more firmly placed on the ground, the woman of a more slender figure, with larger hips and a more ample bosom. The statue of the king which is in the Cairo Museum * was cut in the sandstone with a bold, firm chisel. The feet and knees are thick, the hands massive, the bust indicated in summary fashion, the face boldly modelled. The colour is harsh, the flesh black, the costume white, the cap red, according to the ritual of the ceremonies for which it was destined; the whole has an aspect of barbarism, but a premeditated barbarism, having regard to the religious effect to be produced. If a Memphian sculptor had treated a similar subject, he would not have failed to harmonize the lines and soften the colour: unconsciously he would have fused its type with the softer type of human physiognomy that prevailed in his school, at the risk of enfeebling its energy. The Theban sculptor, on the contrary, exerted himself above all to reproduce the truth as it revealed itself to him, and that preoccupation is dominant to the end with all of his school. They sought the likeness with the intention of exaggerating rather than of softening the individual features of the subject, and in order to attain it, did not shrink from roughness of execution nor violence of colour: they often fell into barbarism, but scarcely ever into banality.

When, under the XIIth Dynasty, Thebes became one of the capitals of Egypt, its kings sometimes employed local artists, sometimes called in sculptors imbued with

* Already published in the *Musée Egyptien*, vol. ii., Pl. IX-X, pp. 25-30.

Studies in Egyptian Art

the Memphian tradition from Heracleopolis or the Fayoum. Chance has preserved for us two colossal heads, one of Sanouosrît I (Ousirtasen),* discovered by Mariette in the ruins of Abydos, the other of Sanouosrît III, extracted by M. Legrain from the pit at Karnak. The handicraft is excellent in both cases, and seldom has this unpromising stone been worked with greater skill, but the inspiration of the whole is different. Here are two persons of the same race, and the general resemblance is sufficient to set aside any doubt: for if it were not there, we should be tempted to see in each a sovereign of a different Dynasty. The first belongs to a school inspired by the Memphian tradition: the sculptor has idealized or, if preferred, symbolized his model, and has given it the short full oval, the smiling good-humoured face that the school adopted for official statues of the Pharaohs. The second, on the other hand, copied the features without softening a single one; the face is long and thin, the brow narrow, the cheek-bones prominent, the jaw bony and heavy. He has hollowed the cheeks, surrounded the nose with two deep furrows, tightened the lower lip and projected it into a contemptuous pout; he has realized a strong work, whereas the other, penetrated by opposite principles, has only evolved from the stone an agreeable composition, but one lacking individuality.

The contrast between the two methods is less striking in the bas-reliefs than in the statues. Among the fragments used by Thoutmôsis III for filling up is a square pillar emanating from a limestone building of

---

* The head was reproduced by Rougé-Banville, "Album photographique," Nos. 111-12 ; cf. Mariette," Monuments divers," Pl. XXI, *a*, *b*, *c*, and p. 299 ; the whole is reproduced in the *Musée Egyptien*, vol. ii., Pl. XIII, and pp. 34-5.

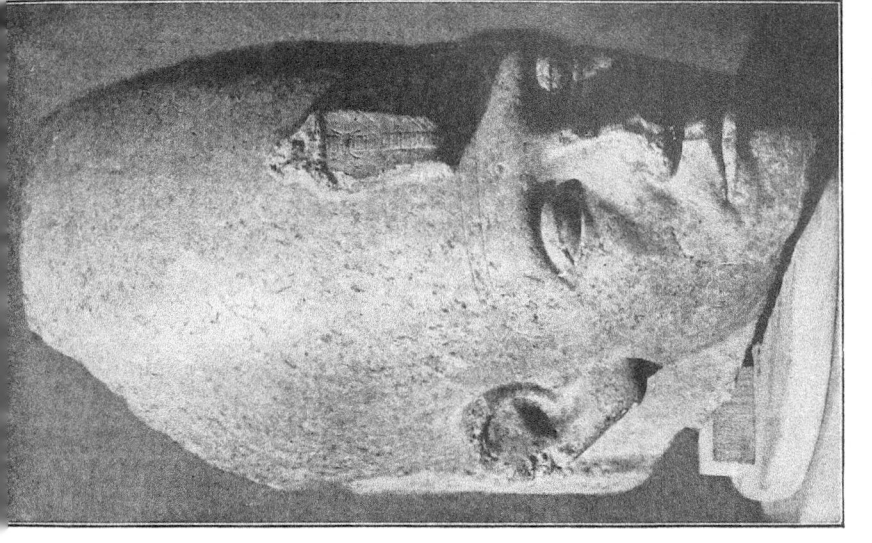

HEAD OF A COLOSSUS OF SANOUOSRÎT.

Pink granite.

MONTOUHOTPOU V.

Painted sandstone.

The Theban School of Sculpture

Sanouosrît I. The Pharaoh is seen on one of the sides accompanied by Phtah. They are there, the sovereign and the god, face to face, breathing each other's breath, according to the etiquette of greeting between persons equal in rank. The style greatly resembles that of the Memphian school, but when examined more closely, peculiarities of the Theban school are to be distinguished. The contours are firmly fixed, the relief is less flat, and consequently the shadows less thin, and thus the outline of the figures stands out more strongly against the background than in the pictures of Gizeh or Saqqarah: a Memphian would perhaps have displayed more elegance, but would have remained true to convention. The scenes engraved on the other three sides also present the characteristics of Theban art, and it is a pity that the fragment is so far unique. If the rest of the temple was decorated in the same happy fashion, the XIVth Dynasty encouraged at Thebes a work comparable to the finest of the XVIIIth or XIXth on the porticoes of Deir-el-Bahari, in the sanctuary of Gournah, and in the Memnonium erected by Setouî I at Abydos.

III

It is with the statues of the XVIIIth Dynasty discovered at Karnak by M. Legrain as with those of the XIIth: directly we look at them we notice distinctive signs of the school, with modifications that are explained when we consider the position of Thebes at that period. The favourite residence of the Pharaohs and permanent seat of their government, its prosperity was continually increased by the booty gained in Syria or Ethiopia, and as wealth increased, so did the taste for

Studies in Egyptian Art

building. Not only did the kings never tire of embellishing the city, but, following their example, private individuals built sumptuous palaces and tombs there. For so much activity a large supply of artists was needed: studios multiplied, sculptors came from all parts of the country to supplement the few Theban sculptors. Those strangers did not join the local school without exercising some influence on it: it was subdivided into several branches, each of which, while preserving a common ground of precepts and habits, soon assumed its personal physiognomy. We already know two or three of them, but how many must there have been during the three centuries that the Dynasty lasted, all the work of which is lost for us or confused with the mass?

I like to attribute to the same studio, besides a certain number of pieces recently acquired by the Cairo Museum, three of the best fragments extricated by M. Legrain from the *favissa*, the Thoutmôsis III, the Isis, and the Sanmaout. The Thoutmôsis III is in a very supple schist that allows the most delicate chiselling, and no engraving can do justice to the delicacy of the modelling: the play of the muscles is discreetly noted, but with extraordinary sureness, and, the imperceptible shadows it produces varying in proportion as we walk round the figure, the aspect of the physiognomy seems to change from moment to moment. Isis was not of royal birth, and perhaps came from one of the lower strata of society: five-and-twenty years ago her existence was not suspected, and the Karnak statue in pink granite is the first portrait we have of her. It is through her, however, that Thoutmôsis III possesses the features by which he differs from his predecessors, the large

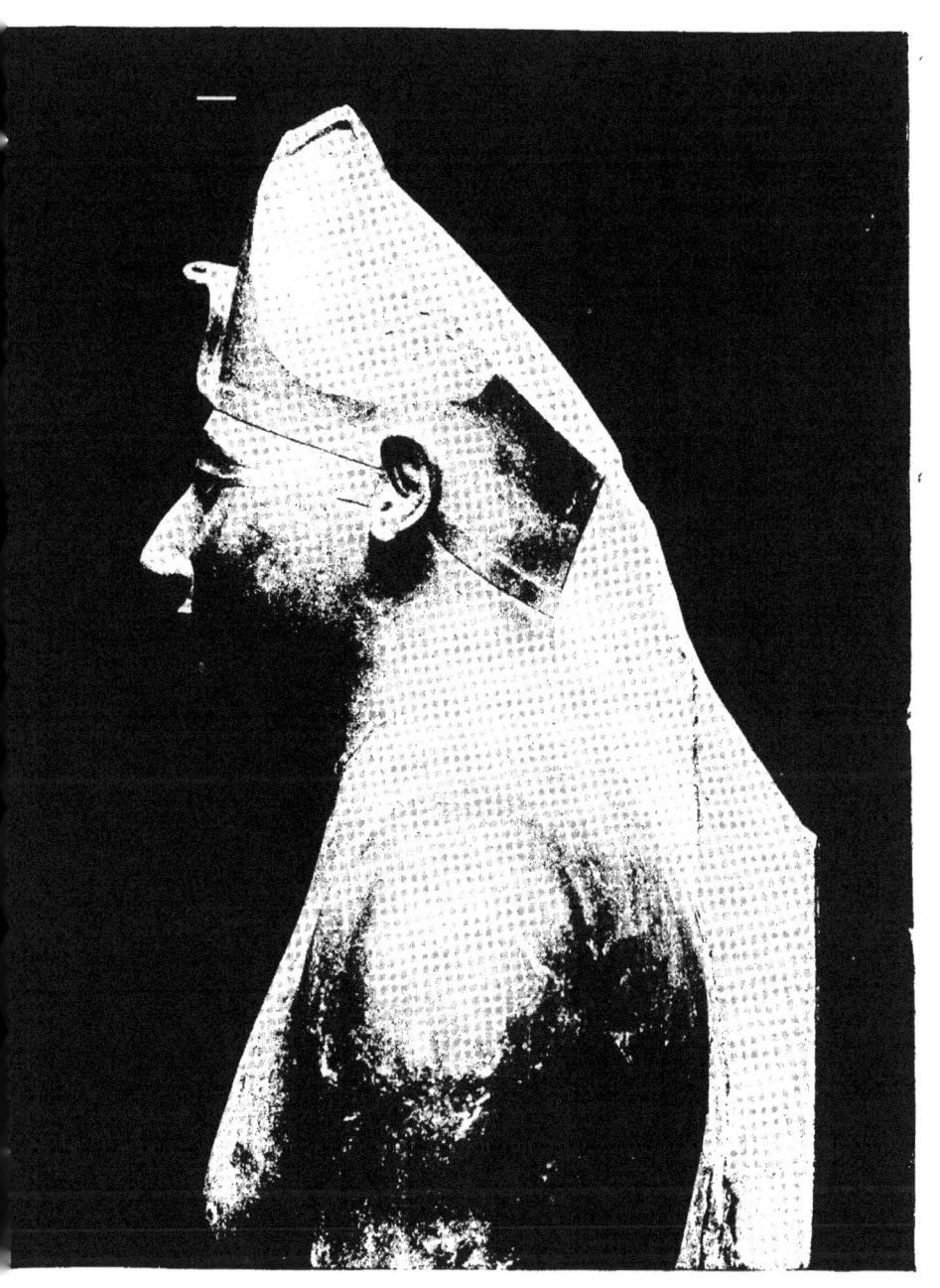

BUST OF THOUTMÔSIS III.
Grey Schist.

ISIS, MOTHER OF THOUTMÔSIS III.

The Theban School of Sculpture

aquiline nose, wide-opened, almost protruding eyes, full mouth, rounded face. The heavy wig he wears made the sculptor's task difficult; so much the greater then is the merit in conceiving a work before which we pause, even by the side of the preceding one. It contains all the characteristics of the Theban school, the seeking after the personal expression, the sincerity of the rendering, the width of the shoulders and, as a set-off, the intentional smallness of the waist between the ample breasts and broad hips. Study of the composition compels us to attribute it to the same studio, if not to the same artist to whom we owe the statue of Thoutmôsis III. I think the same about the group representing Sanmaout and the little princess Nafêrourîya whose steward he was: nothing could be less conventional than the free, firm gesture with which he holds the child, or the posture of trusting abandon with which she leans against his breast. The frankness of the movement well harmonizes with the spiritual gentleness of the face and the smile that animates the eyes and the full lips. Sanmaout was Queen Hachopsouîtou's major-domo, and his sovereign had authorized him to erect his statues in the temple of Amon. After examining those that remain to us, it cannot be doubted that they all come from one of the royal studios, most probably the one whence came later the statues of Thoutmôsis and his mother Isis.

And we have direct proof that the Theban sculptors of that period tried above everything to make sure of the likeness. They drew their subject over and over again before definitely making the rough sketch, and the dry climate of Egypt has preserved many of their cartoons. Cartoon is not exactly the term, since

Studies in Egyptian Art

they used fragments of limestone for their studies, but the word *ostraca* by which they are designated is not much better, and, further, is only intelligible to expert Egyptologists. Hundreds of them have found their way to the Cairo Museum, and they show the attempts of the artist, his hesitations and corrections, the variations of his thought and of his hand, down to the moment when he became absolute master of his model. More than once, too, the chances of excavation have brought the model itself to light, and provided us with the means of comparing the portrait with the original. That is the case with Thoutmôsis III. His mummy was found in 1881 in the *favissa* of Deir-el-Baharî and is exhibited with the others in the Gallery of Sovereigns in the Cairo Museum. The face has certainly greatly changed in course of mummification, and the shrunken flesh, the sunken eyes, the flattened nose, and the discoloured skin make him very different from what he was formerly. But if the superficies has changed, what is beneath has endured: if we compare the profile of the face with the mask of the statue, we must admit that they are identical, with the addition of the life, the expression of which was perpetuated by the sculptor.

Let us skip a century and a half, and transport ourselves to the last years of the Dynasty: they have bequeathed us several pieces that must be related to a common origin: the fine woman's head that Mariette called Taia, the Khonsou and the Amon of Harmhâbi,* the Toutânoukhamanou, and perhaps also the statuette in petrified wood extracted from the *favissa* by Legrain in 1905. Is not a portrait of Aî to be recognized there?

* See article on this group by Legrain in the *Musée Egyptien*, vol. ii., pp. 1–14 and Pl. I–IV.

SANMAOUT AND THE PRINCESS NAFÊROURÎYA
Black granite.

The Theban School of Sculpture

It is broadly treated despite its restricted dimensions, but the unfortunate material employed did not allow the artist to go far as regards execution: the likeness remains uncertain. But it preserves the mark of the school, and various details in the nose, mouth, the cut of the eyes, the inset of the eyebrows, lead me to think that we shall probably be right in attributing it to the group of artists to whom we owe the Khonsou and the Toutânoukhamanou. I am certain that they come from the same hand, and an instant's examination will prove it. The two figures might almost be superimposed: the eye is hollowed out in an identical amount in both, the attachment of the nose is similar, and so is the way of slightly inflating the nostrils and of dilating the middle of the lips and compressing the corners. The physiognomy has something ailing in it, but the indications of ill-health, the obliquity and bruised appearance of the eyes, the thinness of the cheeks and neck, the prominence of the shoulder-bones, are more perceptible in the Khonsou than in the Toutânoukhamanou; we might say that the model of the Khonsou, if it is not Toutânoukhamanou at a more advanced age, had a more visible tendency to consumption. A doctor should study them both: he alone could decide, if, as I imagine, they represent a sick man, and possibly he could, according to the external aspect of the subject, establish the exact diagnosis of the disease.

The similarities are less marked in the head called Taia, and they are not at once noticeable in the engraving: but they are clear to those who have studied the originals. In a slighter degree all the details I have noted in Khonsou and Toutânoukhamanou are there: the queen is not a sick woman, but the different parts of her face are treated in the same way, and the hand which

Studies in Egyptian Art

sculptured them is that which so delicately chiselled the portraits of the god and the Pharaoh, its contemporaries. Even when only the queen was known, her strange physiognomy greatly excited the imagination of scholars. Mariette, who discovered her, thought her a stranger to Egypt; he identified her with Tiyi, the wife of Amenôthes III, and declared her to be Syrian, Hittite, Armenian, and his opinion long prevailed. We know now that her date is at least a quarter of a century after Tiyi, and that she represents the wife or mother of Harmhâbi, one of the Pharaohs who succeeded the heretical sovereigns of the XVIIIth Dynasty. And in fact the portraits of Tiyi that have recently emerged from the earth have no point of likeness with that of Mariette's queen. They present a woman of a thin bony type, with heavy jaw and long depressed chin, a low receding forehead, the physiognomy of the Pharaoh Khouniatonou with which the bas-reliefs and statues of El-Amarna have familiarized us. By the form and expression of her face our queen is allied to the family of Harmhâbi or Toutânoukhamanou: the resemblance of her statue to those of Legrain would sufficiently prove it, if further proof were required.

And now, when the two groups I have just described have been compared, it is easily admitted that the inspiration and technique of the second proceed directly from the inspiration and technique of the first. Taste fluctuated during the five or six generations that divide them, and the caprices of fashion have influenced the execution: but the general characteristics remain unchanged, and their persistence allows us once again to assert the continuity of the school.

STATUETTE IN PETRIFIED WOOD.

THEBAN KHONSOU.

STATUE OF TOUTÂNOUKHAMANOU.

Red granite.

THE SO-CALLED TAIA.

White limestone.

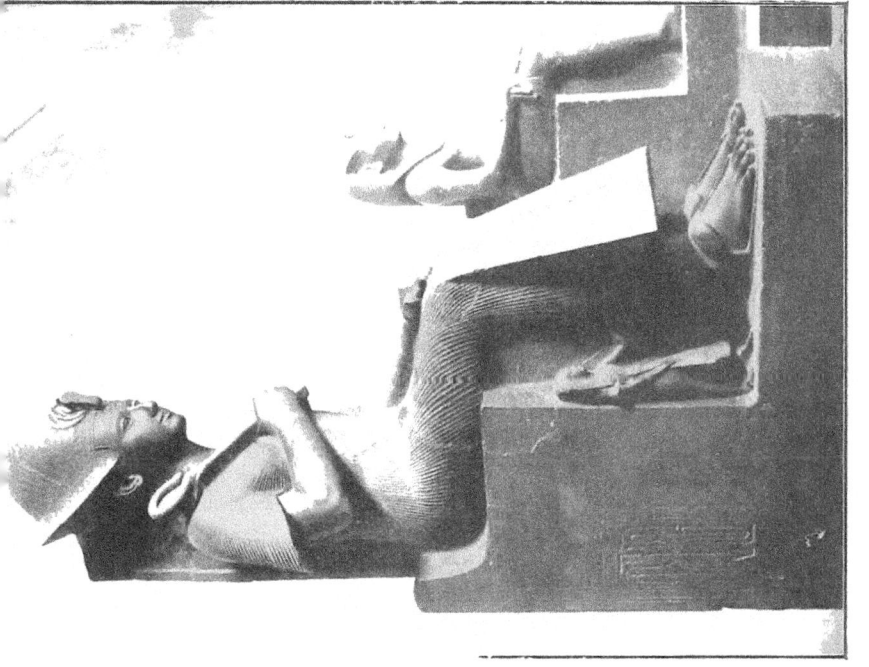

RAMSES II.   RAMSES IV LEADING LIBYAN CAPTIVE.
Alabaster. Turin Museum.

The Theban School of Sculpture

IV.

It maintained its flourishing condition during the XIXth Dynasty, and the *favissa* has restored to us works that yield in nothing to those of the preceding age. In my opinion the best is a mutilated statue of Ramses II, so like the big Turin statue in pose and execution that it might be the first rough draft of it, or the exact smaller copy. A few pieces of the XXth Dynasty are worthy of esteem without rising far above mediocrity, as in a little group in granite of Ramses VI bringing a Libyan prisoner to the god Amon: the bearing of the victorious Pharaoh does not lack pride, the constrained posture of the barbarian is skilfully noted, and the movement of the miniature lion that glides between the two is interpreted with the customary naturalness of the Egyptians when they portray animals.* I prefer the priest with the monkey, or, to give him his name, Ramses-Nakhouîti, the chief prophet of Amon. In a crouching posture, with calves and thighs flat on the ground, a roll spread out before him across his legs, bewigged and petticoated, uncomfortable in his robes of ceremony, with an air of abstraction he meditates, or silently recites prayers to himself. A little hairy cynocephalus perches on his shoulders, and looks at him over his head: it is the god Thot who is revealed in this unusual position, and it was difficult to co-ordinate the beast and the man in a manner that should be neither absurd nor simply ugly. The sculptor has come out with honour. The priest slightly bends his neck, but we feel

* The head of the Pharaoh, which was stolen at the moment of discovery, has been found since this article appeared, and purchased by the Cairo Museum, 1912.

Studies in Egyptian Art

that the beast does not weigh on him: the monkey on his part half shrinks behind the head-dress, and the deep frown of his face prevents the mischievous effect that the countenance of an animal above a human face might have produced. Like the group of Ramses VI, it bears the imprint of the school, but with notable differences of technique: if the first was sculptured in one of the royal studios, the second comes from another studio of which the origin can be indicated.

We know how, about a century after the death of Ramses III, the pontiffs of Amon made themselves masters of the whole of the Thebaïd: while a new Dynasty established itself at Tanis in the eastern delta, they exercised supreme authority over Southern Egypt and Ethiopia, sometimes with the title of high-priest, sometimes with that of king, and their sacerdotal house was the seat of their government. We do not know the exact site, but we learn from an inscription that it was situated near the seventh pylon, not far from the spot where the *favissa* was dug out. It is probable that their relatives obtained the privilege from them, at the moment they assumed domination, of erecting their statues in the temple. The court-yard between the seventh pylon and the hypostyle hall contains only a small number of *ex-votos*: they chose it as the place in which to consecrate their monuments, and filled it in the course of generations. What has come down to us does not include all they erected in their own name or to the memory of those they loved. Many statues were seized or destroyed during civil or foreign wars, but when the Macedonians conquered the land enough remained for more than five hundred to be thrown into the *favissa*. A large number of artists must have been needed to execute so many commissions, and,

THE PRIEST WITH THE MONKEY.

The Theban School of Sculpture

besides its royal studio, Thebes long possessed one or several pontifical studios. To one of those must be assigned the man with the monkey, and nearly all the statues after the fall of the Ramessides. For the most part they have a real value, and scarcely yield to the old royal works, such as the limestone statuette of Orsorkon II, who drags himself along the ground and offers a boat to his god, the fragments of which have disappeared. We are forced to confess, however, that many are, if not bad, of no interest for the history of art.

The usual posture did not lend itself to elegance. They are nearly all crouching, the thighs up to the chest, the arms crossed on the knees: what advantage was to be obtained from an attitude that reduced a man to a mere packet surmounted by a head? Where the model departed from the hieratical posture, the qualities of the school are revealed. The Ankhnasnofiriabrê en Hathor has a somewhat strained gracefulness: it would almost bear comparison with the Amenertaîous so much admired by Mariette, if it were not leaning against a big ugly pillar. Perhaps the contrast between the slender waist and the inflated bust and belly is too marked in the Ankhnas, but the composition of the head is irreproachable. It is nearly always so at that epoch: if the sculptors sometimes neglected the bodies or interpreted them ill, they cared lovingly for the heads. Fine portraits may be counted by the score among the statues found in the *favissa*. I shall only give two here, that of Mantimehê and his son, Nsiphtah, who lived under Taharkou and Psammetichus I. Thebes was then under a curious government. When the male descendants of the priests failed, the power, and those sacerdotal functions that could be exercised by women, passed into the hands

Studies in Egyptian Art

of the princesses: one of them was elected, who, wedded to the god in a mystic marriage, henceforth enjoyed the right of living free as she pleased. To assist them in the government, these *pallacides* of Amon had majordomos, who often filled with them a similar rôle to that of the chief minister with the queens of Madagascar before the occupation of the island by the French. Mantimehê and his son are the best known of these persons, and the artists to whom the care of sculpturing their portraits was entrusted would certainly be the best among those of the sacerdotal studio. It is, in fact, nature itself, and no master of a former age could have expressed better or with a bolder chisel the bustling vulgarity of the father and the aristocratic inanity of the son. The second Saïte period and the beginning of the Greek period are almost entirely unrepresented in the *favissa;* under the Persians, distress was too general for artistic matters to be thought of, and the Macedonian rule had only just been consolidated when the common pit was dug. A granite head, of hasty workmanship but dignified appearance, shows, however, that the Theban studio followed the movement that prevailed in the schools of Lower Egypt, and that, doubtless under the influence of Greek models, it gave attention to details hitherto neglected: the skull is studied with a greater care for accuracy, and also the slight accidents of the physiognomy, the furrows of the forehead, the lines between the eyes and at the rise of the nose, the falling in or puffing out of the cheeks, the play of the muscles round the nostrils and mouth. The sculptor desired to note in his work not only the broad lines of the face, but the small details that characterize the individual and determine his personality.

OSORKON II OFFERING A BOAT TO THE GOD AMON.

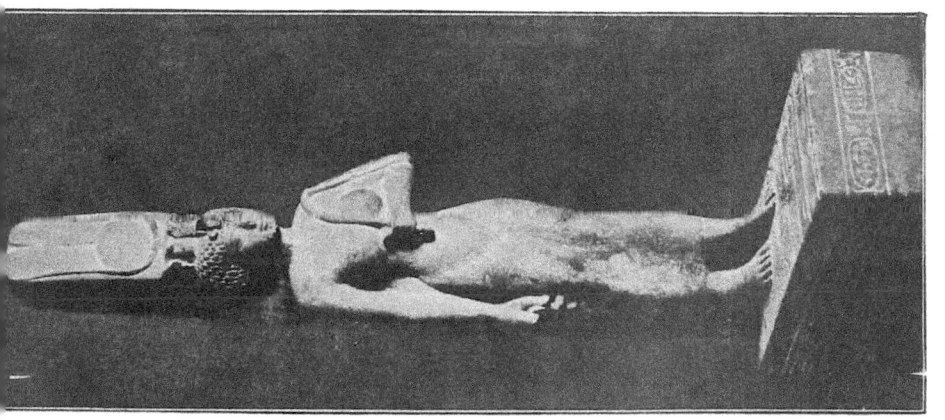

MANTIMEHÊ

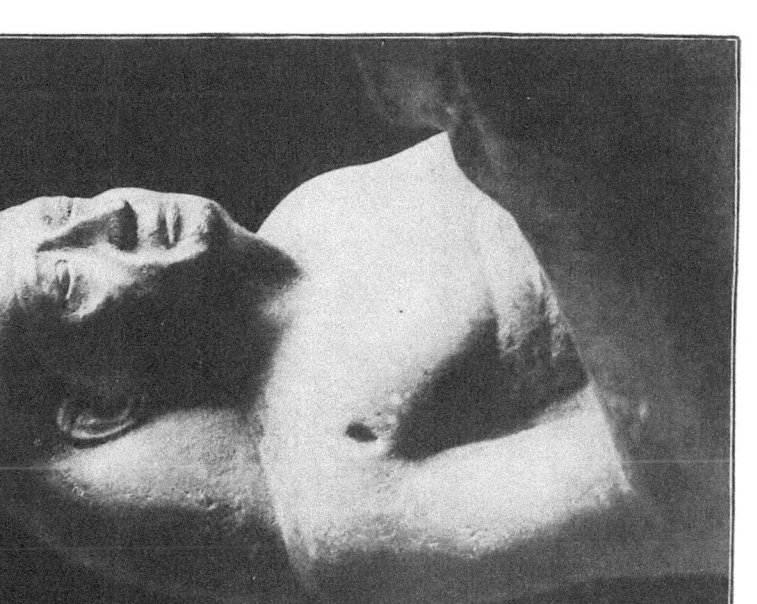

NSIPHTAH, SON OF MANTIMEHĒ

HEAD (SAÏTE PERIOD).

THE COW OF DEIR-EL-BAHARÎ IN HER CHAPEL.

To face p. 104.

The Theban School of Sculpture

V

It is a long time since I undertook to distinguish, under the apparent uniformity with which Egypt is reproached, the varieties of composition and conception that may serve for the recognition of schools, and, in the work of the schools, for that of particular studios. I have not found it difficult to show how the Memphian manner differs from the Theban, nor what distinguishes both from that which flourished at Hermopolis, Tanis, Saïs; but for the lack of sufficiently numerous documents, I had not succeeded in marking out the development of one same school through a long series of centuries. The find at Karnak gave me the materials I lacked, and since M. Legrain has been exploiting it, I have not ceased to search in it for information on that point. I have obtained much there, sometimes, it is true, of varying value, and I have still much to learn both about the most ancient periods and about certain moments of transition in more recent periods. I believe, however, the results already obtained are sufficiently important and significant to compel us to remodel the history of Egyptian art. I have not ventured to do that here, but, short as the present essay is, it may clearly be seen to what results it has led me. I have confirmed the fact that the characteristics of Theban art were those I thought I recognized at the beginning of my studies: I then rapidly noted the stages that the art passed through from the moment that Thebes awoke to political life almost to that when it ceased to exist as a great city.

XI

THE COW OF DEIR-EL-BAHARI *

AT two o'clock in the afternoon of February 12, 1906, while Naville was finishing his lunch, a workman came running up to tell him that the top of a vault was beginning to emerge from the earth. For several days certain indications had led him to think that a discovery was at hand: he went to the spot and at once saw in the mound of sand that dominated the back porticoes of the temple of Montouhotpou a spectacle that filled him with joy. The vault was almost half dug out; under it, in the shade, an admirable cow extended her neck, and seemed to look about her curiously. A few hours' work sufficed to set her completely free. She was intact, but a little figure leaning against her breast had had its face crushed in distant ages, and the violence of the blows had caused a crack in the head and shoulders that compromised its solidity. The chamber that sheltered the cow was built in a hollow of the rock with slabs of sculptured and painted sandstone. The semicircular ceiling did not present the usual regular vault with converging keystones and surfaces ; it was composed of a double row of bent blocks cut in quarters of a circle and buttressed one

* Published in the *Revue de l'Art ancien et moderne*, 1907, vol. xxii., pp. 5-18.

AMENÒTHES II AND THE COW HATHOR.
Three-quarters view.

AMENÔTHES II AND THE COW HATHOR.
(From the right-hand side of the group.)

The Cow of Deir-el-Bahari

against the other at their upper end. It was painted dark blue with yellow five-pointed stars scattered over it to represent the sky. The three vertical partitions were decorated with religious scenes: on the one at the back Thoutmôsis III worships Amonrâ, lord of Thebes, and on the two sides he makes an offering to Hathor, who is no other than the very cow shut into the vault

She was still half buried when some ten inquisitive persons turned their kodaks on her, thus despoiling Naville, and disputing among themselves the pleasure of being the first to photograph her. In the evening nothing else was talked of in the Louxor hotels, and the tourists did not fail to make up parties to go and admire her the next day. The fellahs, on their side, related the most marvellous tales. She had breathed noisily just at the moment that the light of day touched her, and had shivered in all her limbs. She had directed such a look on the workman who had perceived her that he broke his leg with an awkward blow of his axe. She was not, as she seemed to be, of stone, but of fine gold, disguised by Pharaoh's magicians in order to keep off treasure-seekers: a few formulas repeated at a fixed hour with the prescribed fumigations and rites, a little dynamite, and after the explosion the fragments would be transformed into ingots of metal. And as if the sorcerers were not sufficient, dealers in antiquities prowled about in the vicinity. Doubtless she was too heavy for them to think of carrying her off whole, but would they have found it very difficult to detach the head and decamp with it during the night, in spite of the vigilance of our guards or with their complicity? Unscrupulous amateurs are never far to seek, ready to pay heavily for a stolen object, provided they believe it to have an

Studies in Egyptian Art

artistic or archæological value, and the certainty of gaining hundreds of pounds in case of success largely compensates the honest brokers of Louxor for the petty annoyance of disbursing a few pence by way of fine or of undergoing a week's imprisonment if they are caught in the act. I should have preferred to leave the monument in its ancient place, but it would have been tempting fortune, and the only means of saving it was to send it to Cairo. I entrusted the matter to M. Baraize, one of our engineers, and he carried it out extremely well: in less than three weeks he had dismantled the blocks, packed up the cow, and transported the cases by train across the Theban plain. The chapel is now rebuilt in a good position at the end of one of the rooms of the Cairo Museum, but the goddess is not hidden in darkness as at Deir-el-Bahari. She stands at the entrance, her body in the full light, the hinder parts a little under the vault: she comes forth from her house and shows herself freely to visitors, from the snout to the end of the tail.*

II

Our wonder is at first aroused by the mixture she presents of conventional mysticism with realism. The front view shows only the head surrounded by accessories, the significance of which is only appreciated by those who are learned in religious matters. At the top of the composition, between the tall horns in form of a lyre, the usual head-dress of goddess-mothers, is the solar disk flanked

* She is noted in the "Livre d'entrée" under No. 38575 and the chapel under No. 38576.

THE COW HATHOR
Cairo Museum.

The Cow of Deir-el-Bahari

by upstanding feathers and stamped with an inflated uræus. This scaffolding of emblems without thickness and almost without consistence would run the risk of being broken by the slightest blow if it was not supported, and so it rests on two tufts of aquatic plants, the stalks of which, rising from a socket near the hoofs, spring up right and left of the legs; flowers alternating with buds bend over the back of the neck and form a fan-shaped support behind the disk and feathers. Under the snout, and as if framed by the vegetation, is the statuette of a man standing, his back to the cow's chest. As I said, the face is mutilated, the flesh black; he stretches out his hands, palms downward, in front of him with a gesture of submission, as if avowing himself the humble servant of Hathor: by the uræus of the crown and the stiff petticoat spread in a triangle in front of the thighs, we guess him to be a Pharaoh. He is found again in a less punctilious attitude under the right flank of the statue. He is kneeling, naked, and his flesh is red; he presses the teat between his hands, and drinks greedily of the sacred milk. If we may believe the cartouche engraved between the lotuses, the two figures, the black and the red, are one and the same sovereign, Amenôthes II of the XVIIIth Dynasty, and perhaps that is the case. But it was Thoutmôsis III who built the chapel, and it is he that the artists have represented twice over, praying in front of the cow and sucking the udder. It would be strange if, after erecting the sanctuary, he should have omitted to provide it with his goddess. It is more probable that the cow was commissioned by him, and shut up there by his order, but without dedication or cartouche: he considered doubtless that the neighbouring bas-reliefs would constitute sufficient title-deeds. Later, Amenôthes II, wishing to associate himself with his father's

Studies in Egyptian Art

act of piety, and noticing an empty space behind the coiffure, inscribed his name there.

Such a complexity of figures and attributes does not tend to make the appreciation of the work easy for us, and we have also to add the prescriptions of the ritual to the conventions of the craft from which Egyptian artists were never free, at least when stone was their material: the belly, tail, legs, all the lower parts of the group, are enclosed in a stone partition which spoils the effect even while it preserves them from the chances of breakage. And yet, despite defects that shock a sculptor of our time, one glance suffices to reveal the extraordinary beauty of the work. The head differs from that of our European cows, but it is a question of race, and whoever has seen the Soudanese cow of the present day will easily distinguish its features in the Hathor of Deir-el-Baharî: the fullness of the brow, the subtle modelling of the temples and cheeks, the gentle widening out of the snout, the suppleness of the nostrils, and the smallness of the mouth. Such accuracy of detail will delight the naturalist, but it might be feared that it would harm the artistic value of the whole. That is not the case at all, and if at a distance the physiognomy seems to have only an expression of gentleness and meditative somnolence, as soon as we go near it assumes an air of intelligent attention. The eye seems to grow larger and to follow the visitor who arrives, the snout to contract and palpitate, as if to scent out. The sculptor, instead of following the tradition and polishing the stone as highly as possible, has respected the fine furrows of the chisel, and the light playing on them gives at moments the illusion of a shudder running over the skin. The body is of equally accurate composition, the chest narrow, shoulders thin, spine long and saddle-backed, leg

The Cow of Deir-el-Bahari

long and slender, the thigh sinewy, the haunches prominent, the udder only slightly developed. The hinder part is worked with an incredible fidelity. Contrary to custom, the coat is red-brown, darker on the back, lighter, of a tawny shade that becomes white, on the belly; it is speckled with black spots, like flowers with four petals, which we should consider artificial, if there were not animals of Soudanese origin in the Egyptian herds of to-day that show similar markings. By those spots they recognize among the heifers of the year the one in which Hathor has deigned to become incarnated, and which must be worshipped as long as she remains on earth.

III

She was, above all, the divinity of the dead. The buildings scattered about that corner of the necropolis were not exclusively consecrated to the gods of the living; they were the chapels attached to royal tombs, some of which, like that of Montouhotpou, were contiguous to the tomb, while others, like that of Queen Hachopsouîtou, for example, were relegated to the other side of the mountain, in the Bibân-el-Molouk. The sovereigns were sometimes praying and bringing offerings to the gods, sometimes associated with them and taking part in their sacrifices. Hathor, ruler of the West and lady of the heaven, had become by a concourse of ideas, the reasons of which can be understood, the mistress of souls and *doubles*: she played thus a part of great importance in places where the worship of her vassals was celebrated. Walk through the halls of the large terraced temple and you will find her repeatedly with the figure and posture assumed by her in the oratory discovered by Naville: she

Studies in Egyptian Art

is the foster-mother whose milk Thoutmôsis and Hachopsouîtou are greedily imbibing. The suckling of the sovereign was not a mere metaphor of language, realized and transcribed on stone, but a material act borrowed from the customs of Egyptian law, and the final formality of the ceremonies of the adoption. The woman who had no son to perpetuate her memory, and desired to have one, after reading the preliminary passages, had to offer one of her breasts, in all probability the right, to the youth or man she had chosen; he would press the teat between his lips for a few seconds, and by this pretence of feeding would become to her as a son. Among half civilized peoples where this custom prevails, it is not required that the woman has been or is still married: only, the young girl who acquires a child by this method covers her breast with a thin stuff before going through the ceremony. If, then, Thoutmôsis III, or by usurpation Amenôthes II, was represented kneeling under the right teat of the Hathor, he wished thereby to prove that she was his divine mother, and the complacent manner in which she yields him her milk sufficiently shows that she admitted the legitimacy of his claim.

But these are only half the ideas expressed by the group, and it remains for us to determine the meaning of the flowering lotuses which stand at the right and left. As sovereign of the West and of the lands in which the dead sojourned, she assumed different forms according to the provinces. In the North the people imagined her under the aspect of one of those fine sycamores which grow in the midst of the sand on the borders of the Libyan Desert, rendered green and thick by the hidden waters sent them by the infiltrations of the Nile. The mysterious path which leads to the shores of the West

AN UNKNOWN FIGURE AND THE COW HATHOR.

The Cow of Deir-el-Baharî

brings the *doubles* to her feet; as soon as they are arrived, the divine soul, lodged in the trunk, thrust out the half or the whole of her body, and offered them a vase full of pure water and a tray filled with loaves. If they accepted her gifts—and they could scarcely refuse them—they confessed at once that they were her vassals; they were no longer authorized to return to the living, but the regions of the world beyond the tomb would open to them. In the nomes of the Said where she was imagined to be a cow, she haunted a fertile marsh situated on the slopes of the Libyan mountains; whenever a *double* came to its edge she stretched forth her head from among the herbage to meet him, and claimed his homage, and when he had paid it, she allowed him to enter the realms of the funereal gods. The 186th Chapter* of the "Book of the Dead," a very favourite one with devout persons under the second Theban Empire, initiates us into this myth, and the vignette that precedes it shows us the scene as the Egyptians conceived it: the red or yellow slopes of the mountain, the tufts of aquatic plants, the cow conferring with the defunct. The Pharaoh who commissioned our group—or rather the sculptor who executed it—combined the idea common to all with the royal concept of the adoption by the goddess, and he expressed the result therefrom as completely as the processes of his art permitted. He reduced the marsh to two slender clusters of lotus, and marked the two chief points of the adoption by means of two little royal figures and their attributes. The first, as we have seen, wears the costume of the Pharaohs and has black flesh; standing upright under the animal's snout, it faces the spectator. Amenôthes II has just arrived in front of

* Naville, "Das Thebanische Todtenbuch," vol. i., Pl. CCXXII.

Studies in Egyptian Art

the cow and addressed to her the prayer in which he conjures her to aid him in his journey in search of the everlasting cities; his colour indicates that he is still the slave of death, but the goddess has already enrolled him among her adherents, and presents him to the universe as her well-beloved son. That formality over, he slips through the verdure, kneels down, and crushing the teat in his hand, greedily puts his lips to it. That is the final rite of the adoption, and also the pledge of his return to normal existence. Scarcely has he swallowed the first mouthfuls of milk than life enters his veins; the artist has represented him naked as a new-born infant, and painted his flesh red, the colour of the living.

IV

The two forms of Hathor welcoming the dead are not each confined to the province in which it was born. They gradually spread over the whole country, not without experiencing diverse fortunes. Hathor in the tree was reserved for papyri, stelæ, and bas-reliefs. The first idea was scarcely suitable for statuary, and the cleverest sculptor would have been embarrassed to derive a large tree from the stone, a goddess lost in the branches, a person in prayer before the tree and before the goddess. But it lent itself to painting, and some of the vignettes in which it is expressed in the excellent copies of the "Book of the Dead" or on the walls of the Theban hypogeums, show us the admirable way in which the designers of the new empire used it. Nothing could be more varied or skilful than the relations they establish between the woman and the sycamore on the one hand and the dead person on the other. He is sometimes accompanied by

PETESOMTOUS AND THE COW HATHOR.

The Cow of Deir-el-Bahari

his soul, a big hawk with human head and arms, which mimics his slightest gestures : while the *double* receives the elixir of youth in his clasped hands, the soul turns a runnel aside for his own benefit, and greedily drinks from it. Colour adds its charm to the composition, and the replicas of the subject to be seen at Cheîkh Abd-el-Gournah in the hypogeums of the XVIIIth and XIXth Dynasties would obtain a place of honour in our museums, if it was permitted to detach them and mount them in separate panels.

Hathor in the marshes was entirely suited to the ordinary conditions of sculpture, and if in some places serious difficulties were presented, I have indicated how the Theban masters overcame them. She provided a fairly frequent theme for the studios, and the Cairo Museum possesses three examples. They are smaller than the Deir-el-Bahari group, and do not unite the two concepts of the adoration and the adoption. Consequently the lotus is wanting and the dedicatory figure at the cow's udder. They are the affair of simple private persons who had no right to proclaim themselves children of the goddess. If they had attempted to touch the breast of Hathor they would have usurped one of the privileges of royalty; they appear then only once in each group, standing or crouching in front of the chest. In one, which is in grey schist and measures nearly four and a half feet long, the donor has lost his head and neck, and he lifts up a table of offerings with both hands in front of him; the cow also is decapitated.* No trace of inscription is to be seen on the pedestal, but the composition is that of

---

* It comes from Tell Tmai, and is entered in the "Livre d'entrée" under No. 38930, and in the "Guide to the Museum," 3rd English edition, under No. 461, p. 164.

Studies in Egyptian Art

the first Saïte period. The piece, although not the most mediocre that could be found, lacks originality; it is the work of a skilful journeyman who had no personal inspiration, and only knew how to apply the formulas of the school conscientiously. The second group is in yellowish limestone. It measures not quite three feet in length and has suffered more than the preceding one.* Not only has the animal's head been destroyed, but its tail and one of its hind legs have vanished. The man is mutilated to the point that only one of his feet remains to prove to us that he was kneeling. He bore a table of offerings. An inscription engraved on the edge of the pedestal informs us that he was called Petesomtous, and the name, together with the style, takes us back to the Saïte period, perhaps to the period of the Persian domination. The composition is, besides, sufficiently rough, and it would not deserve any attention if the interest of the subject did not compensate for its insignificance as a work of art.

The third was celebrated from the moment of its discovery. It is in green schist, slightly over three feet in length, and under it in height. It was found by Mariette at Saqqarah, fifty years ago, in the tomb of a certain Psammetichus, a contemporary of the first Nectanebo.† It was accompanied by two fine statues of Osiris and Isis,‡ which are the glory of the Cairo Museum, and we owe them for a certainty to the same artist. The

---

* No. 38932 in the "Livre d'entrée"; cf. "Notice des principaux monuments du Musée de Gizeh," 1893, p. 86, and No. 683 of Borchardt's unpublished catalogue. The monument comes from Saqqarah.

† "Guide to the Cairo Museum," 3rd edition, pp. 331–33, No. 1020; "Livre d'entrée," No. 38927.

‡ Guide to the Cairo Museum," 3rd edition, p. 330, Nos. 1018, 1019; "Livre d'entrée," Nos. 38928, 38929.

PSAMMETICHUS AND THE COW HATHOR.
Three-quarters view.

The Cow of Deir-el-Bahari

posture of the cow is the same as that of Deîr-el-Baharî; like her, the head-dress is formed of the solar disk with the uræus surmounted by two long feathers, but a *monaît* fastened round the neck by its chain lies flat on the spine. Psammetichus stands under the head, his back to the chest, his hands hanging down over the apron, with the same gesture of submission as that of Amenôthes II. Besides his name and protocol, the inscriptions contain a prayer for his happiness, addressed to the benevolent Hathor. The hardness of the material has prevented the sculptor from completely freeing the fragile parts: the cow's legs and belly are sunk in the stone, as are the back and feet of the man; the head-dress is supported by a semi-cone set in the back of the neck, and the ears are reinforced by a pad which doubles their thickness. The sculptor, embarrassed by the necessity of preserving masses of superfluous material, had the ingenious idea of treating the lower limbs as a bas-relief. He has designed them on each side of the panel that supports the belly, so that Hathor has two chest profiles and a double supply of legs. He has so cleverly arranged this superabundance of legs that it is not noticeable at a first glance, and some effort of thought is required to make sure that it exists. But despite these eccentricities the work is of rare perfection. Never has such hard stone been manipulated with greater suppleness; the outlines have a harshness that all the virtuosity of the execution has not been able to prevent, but the modelling of the bodies and the faces, both of the animal and of the man, is of unparalleled delicacy, and the whole breathes serenity mingled with melancholy. It is, as a piece of animal sculpture, the best that has come down to us in Saïte art.

Studies in Egyptian Art

V

Nevertheless, it loses when compared with the schist group of the time of Amenôthes II. The mythological element is less predominant, and the head gains by not being framed by two tufts of aquatic plants: but if the religious convention is less encumbering, the artistic convention and the conventions of the studio come out in a much more apparent fashion. The Saqqarah group belongs to the Memphian school, and, as with nearly all the products of that school, the form has something artificial and impersonal. Hathor is a symbolic cow, the half-abstract type of Egyptian cows, a type that in the eyes of the Memphians realized the ideal of the earthly or sacred cow: she has the elegance, but also the softness and the rather insipid meekness, which distinguishes the human figures. The Hathor of Naville, on the contrary, belongs to the Theban school, and possesses the characteristics that I have described above.* The royal studio whence it came was governed by the theological laws, and was forbidden to modify in any way the types that, in the course of ages, had been determined on for revealing the concepts of popular tradition or learned dogma, but it tried to keep their expression as near to life as the rites authorized. The artist who produced the Memphian Hathor chose a pattern from his cartoons, and translated it into stone without troubling to correct the banal purity by imitating a beast of the sacred herd. The sculptor to whom we owe the Theban Hathor, on the contrary, while preserving the ritual arrangement of the parts and the accumulation of the symbols, has placed them on a real

* See the *Revue*, 1906, vol. xx., pp. 241-52, and pp. 337-46 ; and pp. 90-105 of the present volume.

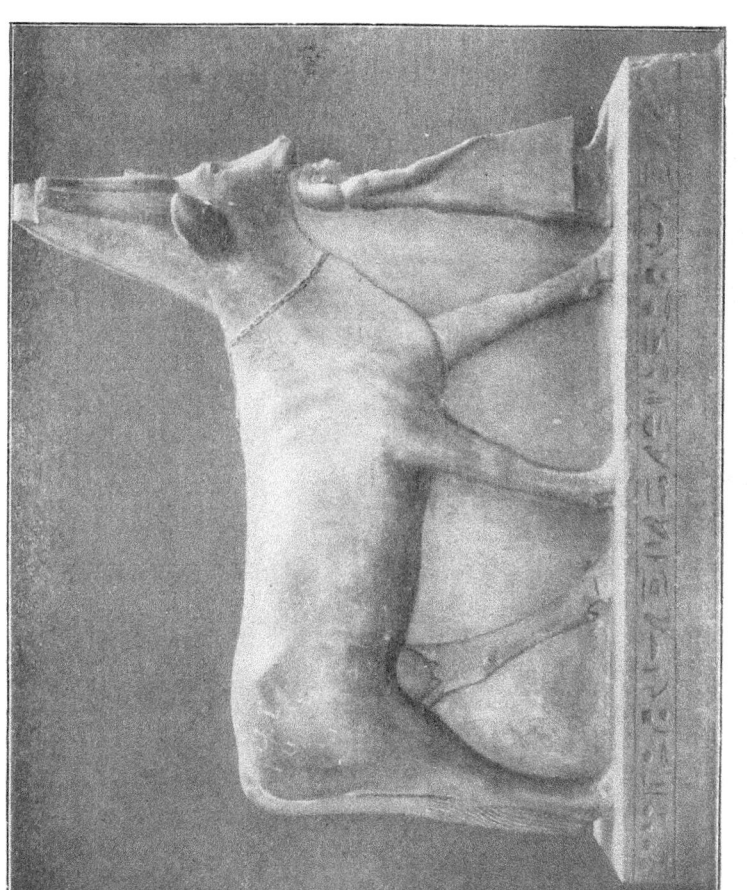

PSAMMETICHUS AND THE COW HATHOR.
From the right-hand side of the group.

The Cow of Deir-el-Bahari

cow, on the cow, perhaps, that for the moment incarnated the goddess in the neighbouring temple of Queen Hachopsouîtou. Imagine her without the emblematic surroundings he was compelled to give her—the heavy head-dress, the lotus tufts, the two statuettes of the Pharaoh—and you will have the good motherly creature who goes peaceably to pasture, and, as she goes, observes everything with her eye, inquisitive and dreamy at the same time. Neither Greece nor Rome has left us anything that can be compared with it; we must go to the great sculptors of animals of our own day to find an equally realistic piece of work.

XII

THE STATUETTE OF AMENÔPHIS IV

(*The Louvre*)

THE statuette originally formed part of a group. The lower part has been fairly skilfully restored in modern times: the upper comes from the Salt collection,* and, like most of the objects of that collection, was found at Thebes. It represents Amenôphis IV of the XVIIIth Dynasty, the first in date of the Pharaohs we are accustomed to name the heretic kings.

In making only a cursory examination we are struck by the ways in which it differs from the royal statuettes that have come down to us. The Pharaohs are usually seated with the head erect, the bust firm, in a posture of stiff dignity which did not lack grandeur. Here the royal stiffness has almost wholly disappeared. The head leans slightly forward, the bust sinks down, it seems as if the body, powerless to hold itself up, is going to slip off the seat; the abandon of the posture is in entire harmony with the character of the person. The back is slightly rounded, the hips are larger than are suitable for a man, the belly and chest inflated; the breasts are round like those of a woman, the puffed-out

* It was catalogued by Champollion in his " Notice descriptive des monuments égyptiens du Musée Charles X," Paris, 1827, p. 55, No. 11.

AMENÔPHIS IV.
The Louvre.

Amenôphis IV

torso is wrinkled in folds of fat, the face is weak and good-natured. In all that, the artist has set aside the æsthetic rules usual in Egypt. If it were not for the awkward angle formed by the arm that holds the sceptre and the whip, and the bad execution of the hand that rests on the left thigh, his work might be quoted as an excellent specimen of what a conscientious sculptor could do at the best moments of Theban art between Thoutmôsis III and Setouî I.

I do not believe that in the long series of Pharaohs there is a prince who has been so badly treated by contemporary scholars as he has been, and about whom they have allowed greater rein to their imagination. At first, the roundness of his body and the exaggeration of his breast caused him to be taken for a woman: for a long time Champollion characterized him as a queen, and was only convinced of his error with difficulty. Later, Mariette thought he recognized in him the exterior signs of a eunuch. Contemporary monuments assign him a wife and children, and we can find a way of reconciling this embarrassing posterity with the new theory. It suffices to suppose that, after having been married and become the father of four daughters, he went to war with one of those African tribes that have preserved to this day the custom of castrating their prisoners: having fallen into their hands, he would have left them as we see him. Some Egyptologists have accused him of being an idiot, the more moderate only regard him as a fanatic. Born of a foreign mother, the white Taia, brought up by her to worship Canaanitish deities, he had scarcely ascended the throne before he wished officially to replace the worship of Amon by that of the solar disk, whose Egyptian name, Aton, perhaps reminded him of the Syrian

Studies in Egyptian Art

name Adoni or Adonaï. This story is well imagined, but to me it seems more than doubtful. Two proofs have been advanced concerning the foreign origin of Taîa: the pink colour of her cheeks and the curious form of the names used in her family. The flesh of Egyptian women was always painted pale yellow: if Taia is pink, it is because she was fairer than they, and consequently of exotic birth. The argument was specious, but it is not permissible to repeat it to-day. For it has been discovered that in the time of Amenôphis II and Amenôphis III the artists for some years employed pink tones for the flesh of their personages, both men and women, and the confirmation of that fact takes away any value from the reasoning deduced from Taîa's colour. Taia has pink flesh in the monuments because the fashion of the day required that she should so have it, and not because she possessed the fair complexion of the northerner. As to the names of the members of her family, Iouaa, Touaa, they do not seem to me to be Asiatic. Doubtless they are not constructed in the Theban manner, but they are found, and many like them, in the tombs of the Ancient Empire. Far from proving a Canaanitish or Libyan extraction, they take us back to the oldest periods of the history of Egypt and denote a Memphian or Heliopolitan origin.

If, as everything indicates, Taia is not a foreigner, we no longer have any cause to seek beyond Egypt for the motives that made Amenôphis IV decide to proscribe the worship of Amon. In fact, the religion of Aton that he professed is indigenous in its formulas and ceremonies. Aton is the solar disk, the shining globe lighted every morning in the east in order to be extinguished every evening in the west; for some theologians it was the

Amenôphis IV

visible body in which Râ, the solar god *par excellence*, was the soul; for others the actual god, and not the shining manifestation of the god. The Theban priesthood had adopted the first theory, which better harmonized with its monotheistic tendencies, and it had developed it to the utmost: it had fused together all the forms of the divinity, and only recognized in it the aspects, the diverse conditions of one and the same being who was the soul of the Sun, Amonrâ. The schools of Memphis and Heliopolis, older than those of Thebes, had remained more closely attached to the ancient polytheism, and interpreted its doctrines in a more material sense. A fact that, so far, no one has ever brought forward, proves incontestably that the worship rendered by Amenôphis IV to Aton was connected with that of the sun as practised at Heliopolis: the high priest of Aton, the supreme head of the royal religion, bore the same official name and the same titles as that of Râ at Heliopolis.

If, however, the monuments tell us that the worship of Aton was a form of the most ancient worship of Râ, they do not so far assist us to determine the points of detail in which it differed. The solar disk of Amenôphis IV, the supreme god Aton, is recognized by the rays terminating in hands that he darts on the earth: the hands brandish the anserated cross, and bring life to everything that exists. I am not sure that Amenôphis IV invented this imagery: I like to think that in that, as in everything, he was bound to follow tradition. The prayers that accompany the figure of the god, the ceremonies celebrated in his name, are all Egyptian; they present that character of seriousness and sometimes of licence to be observed at Denderah, and in all the places where the sombre myth of dead Osiris does not rule. The bas-reliefs that have preserved its physiognomy for us might serve as an illustration for the picture drawn by Herodotus of the great festival of Bubastis.

Having said that, it may be asked what motives impelled Amenôphis IV to deny the gods of his forefathers and to embrace a Heliopolitan religion. It should be noted at once that his father, Amenôphis III, had already set the example of a special affection for solar worships other than that of Amon: we may then believe that Amenôphis IV as a child was brought up in particular devotion for Râ, and that later, a natural result of his early education, he was desirous of imposing his favourite deity on his subjects. But I do not think that religious faith was the sole, or even the principal reason of his cruel persecution of the priests and partisans of Amon; politics probably were chiefly responsible. Amon was, above all, the patron of Thebes: he had made the greatness of the Theban Dynasties, and they, in their turn, had exalted him above all his compeers. The conquests in Syria and Ethiopia had not been without benefit for Egypt in general, but they had been specially advantageous to Amon; the greater part of the booty had passed into his coffers, his priests filled the public offices, and his chief prophet was the highest personage of the empire after the reigning sovereign. Had there been under Thoutmôsis IV an attempt similar to that which delivered the last Ramessides to the pontiffs of Amon and which raised Hrihor to the throne? I do not know; but I believe the desire to counterbalance their power weighed heavily in the favour shown by Amenôphis III to other divinities, and that a definite wish to overturn not only Amon, but especially his clergy, induced Amenôphis IV to thrust Aton into the first rank. He

Amenôphis IV

did not recoil from any means that would lead to success. As the destiny of Amon was indissolubly bound up with that of Thebes, so long as Thebes was the capital, Amon and his priests would keep the supremacy. Amenôphis IV, after changing his name, which was a profession of faith in the excellence of Amon, for that of Khounaton, "splendour of Aton," founded a new capital which he called the city of Aton; he installed there a new priesthood which he richly endowed, and then erased the name of Amon from all the monuments throughout Egypt and even at Thebes. But the worship of Amon had its roots too deeply implanted in the land, and his priests were too powerful, for the king to prevail against them. When he was dead, his successors gave up the struggle: Aton returned into obscurity, his city was deserted, and the name of the king, proscribed by sacerdotal hatred, vanished with the buildings on which it had been engraved.

His attempt was not without influence on art. The necropolis of El-Amarna has told us the names of two of the sculptors who helped to adorn the city during its brief existence. Their works are distinguished from earlier ones by a greater freedom of composition, and particularly by greater realism in the reproduction of the persons. The Amenôphis IV of the Louvre does honour to their talent; it is the more valuable since their works, treated with great ferocity by the Theban reaction, have become very rare. We have a certain number of bas-reliefs more or less mutilated, but very few statues; that of the Louvre is, so far, a unique work of its kind.

XIII

FOUR CANOPIC HEADS FOUND IN THE VALLEY OF THE KINGS AT THEBES*

AMONG the principal objects discovered by Theodore Davis in 1907 in the Valley of the Kings, in the secret chamber where the heretic Pharaoh Khouniatonou was buried with an equipment partly consisting of objects that had belonged to his mother, Tiyi, there are four alabaster Canopic jars of a rare perfection even for that period of perfect execution. The body of the jar is a little longer than is usual, slender at the base, bulging out at the top, with a polish at once unobtrusive and pleasing to the eye. An inscription had been engraved on it, and so far as may be judged by the place it occupied, was the ordinary dedication to the deities protecting the entrails; but it has been effaced, then the place smoothed over, and tinted with the colour of the surrounding part. The touching up is accomplished with so much skill that we can only here and there, beneath the transparence of the glazing, guess at a few marks of the old writing. The four lids are in the form of a human head, a very refined head framed in the short wig with close rows of little flat locks of hair: a golden uræus, now vanished, stood on the

* Published in the *Revue de l'Art ancien et moderne*, 1910, vol. xxviii., pp. 241-52.

KING KHOUNIATONOU.
Alabaster Canopic head found at Thebes.

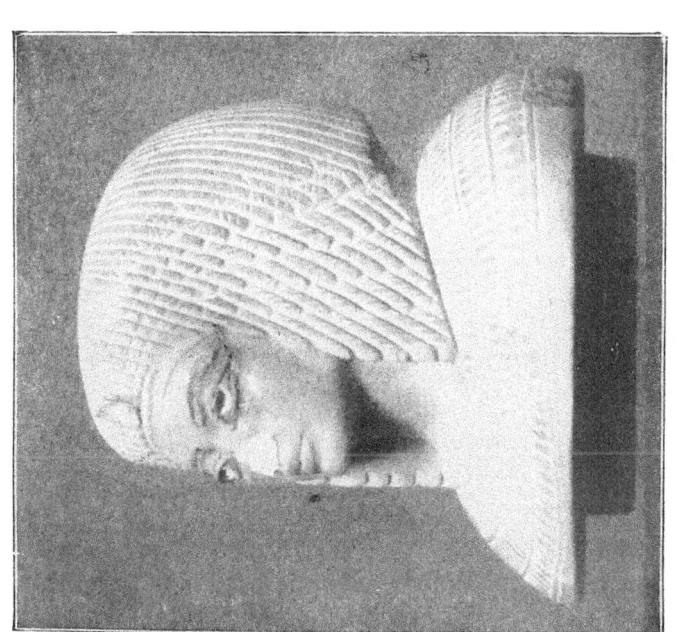

KING KHOUNIATONOU.
Alabaster Canopic head found at Thebes.

Four Canopic Heads

forehead. As the face is beardless, and the whole of the equipment except the coffin bears the name of Tiyi, the Canopic jars have been attributed to the queen. I do not share that opinion; I maintain that they belonged to the Pharaoh, and that we should see his authentic portrait in them.

No one who has seen the four heads side by side will doubt that they represent one and the same person. The insignificant differences to be noticed between them are caused by unimportant technical details, or by breakages in the stone, or by the action of damp, or the different way in which time has treated the materials of which the eyes were formed. The eyebrows consist of a fillet of blue enamel encrusted on the edge of the arch, and the eye, properly so-called, is also designated by a blue fillet, which includes a cornea in white limestone, relieved with red at the corners, and an iris of black stone. In some, the eyebrow is gone. In others the iris has fallen, leaving blind one or both the eyes, or, the whole having been displaced, the eye has been brought forward as if the person was suffering from the beginning of an exophthalmic goitre. Very different expressions of countenance are the result, but under them all the same face is quickly recognized: a longish oval, rather thin at the bottom, a somewhat narrow forehead, a straight nose, thin where it joins the face and turned up at the end almost like Roxelana's, delicate wide-opened nostrils, the sides thin and nervous, a short upper lip, a small but full mouth, a bony chin, pointed and heavy, joined to the neck by a rather harsh line. None of the heads have been entirely respected by time, and one of them has lost its nose, but by good luck, rare in archæology, the best in composition is also that which has suffered least: if the enamel of

Studies in Egyptian Art

the eyelids is wanting, the eyes are intact and the epidermis without scratches. I do not think that there exists in the Egyptian sculpture of that period a more energetic or living physiognomy: the mouth is closed as if to retain the words that desire to escape, the nostrils are inflated and palpitate, the eyes look keenly and frankly into those of the visitor. With age, the alabaster has taken on the dull complexion of the great Egyptian ladies, always protected by the veil, which the sun can never burn. So that it is not surprising that many should have felt in looking at them that they were heads of a woman, and, knowing the circumstances of the discovery, imagined that they saw the most celebrated woman there had then been in the Egyptian Empire, the queen-dowager Tîyi.

Strictly speaking, that is quite possible, for on the one hand the head-dress and necklace into which the neck fits are common to both sexes, and on the other, the features, more accentuated than is usual with a woman, are not so to the point of only fitting a man; directly, however, they are compared with those of the portraits of Tiyi, we are bound to confess that the resemblance is slight. Two types of these have come down to us. In the first, which is by far the most frequent, her face was remodelled and symbolized in the studios of Thebes in accordance with the customary formula for queens. The colossal group of Medinet Habou, recently transported to the Cairo Museum, offers, perhaps, the best example. There, following the regulations, Tiyi is furnished with a round, regular face, almond-shaped eyes, good cheeks, straight nose, smiling mouth, and normal chin: there is something about her which prevents us from confusing her with the other princesses of her era, but she has pre-

KING KHOUNIATONOU.
Alabaster Canopic head found at Thebes.

Four Canopic Heads

served none of the peculiarities that compose her actual physiognomy. That is no longer the case with the most individual of the specimens of the second type, the soapstone head that Petrie discovered at Sinaï, which is now in the Cairo Museum. The right wing of the wig is wanting, and the nose has been crushed by an unfortunate blow on the left nostril, without, however, losing anything of its essential form; a cartouche engraved on the front of the head-dress tells us the name, and at the first glance the portrait gives the impression of a good likeness. It is not flattering. If we are to believe it, Tiyi presented the racial characteristics of the Berbers or of the women of the Egyptian desert: small eyes puckered at the temples, a nose with a broad tip and contemptuous nostrils, a heavy, sulky mouth with turned-down corners, the lower lip dragged back by a receding chin like that of a semi-negress: the receding chin alone forbids us to identify her with the original of our Canopic jars. They have certainly a family likeness, and it could not be otherwise, for if I am right it is a question of mother and son, but variations are to be noted in the son which remove him from the type so clearly revealed in Petrie's statuette. That type, on the contrary, is preserved intact in the admirable head in painted wood which has passed into the collection of Herr Simon of Berlin. We might even say that it is exaggerated, and that the eyes are more oblique, the cheek-bones more prominent, the nose more aggressive, the smiling muscles more sharply evident, the mouth and chin closer to that of a negress. I believe it to be one of Tîyi's granddaughters who became queen after the fall of the Heretic Dynasty: her head-dress, which was originally that of a private person, was afterwards modified to receive the insignia of royalty.

Studies in Egyptian Art

Was she married to Harmhâbi, to Ramses, or to Setouî I? The deviation between the group to which she belongs and that of the Canopic jars is sufficiently great to force us to give up the idea that they represent one person. In addition, our Canopic sculptures possess only one uræus on the forehead, as is customary with kings, while the others have the double uræus which then begins to be the etiquette with queens. That rule has exceptions, and therefore I shall not deduce too strict conclusions from it: but the absence of the second uræus is not less a somewhat strong presumption in favour of the opinion that our Canopic heads are those of a man and not of a woman.

If, however, they are portraits of a man, the circumstances of their discovery compel us to declare that he must be the king Khouniatonou; but how are we to be convinced of this when we remember the grotesque silhouette that the sculptors of El-Amarna have given him? To believe them, he would have been physically a sort of degenerate, tall, weakly, with hips and chest like a woman's, a neck without consistency, an absurd head, a flat, almost non-existent forehead, an enormous nose, an ugly mouth, a massive chin.* He seems to have liked these caricatures, and his friends, imitating him from a desire to flatter him, altered more or less the shape of their own bodies in order that they might resemble that of his. Documents of different origins prove, however, that he was not, or had not always been, the queer figure that is attributed to him. The Louvre alone possesses two such witnesses. The first, which came to the Museum in its early days, is a charming statuette in yellow soapstone. The king is seated, but he has lost the bottom of the legs, which a modern restorer has skilfully replaced. He wears

* See pp. 120–125.

KING KHOUNIATONOU.
Alabaster Canopic head found at Thebes.

KING KHOUNIATONOU.
Cairo Museum.

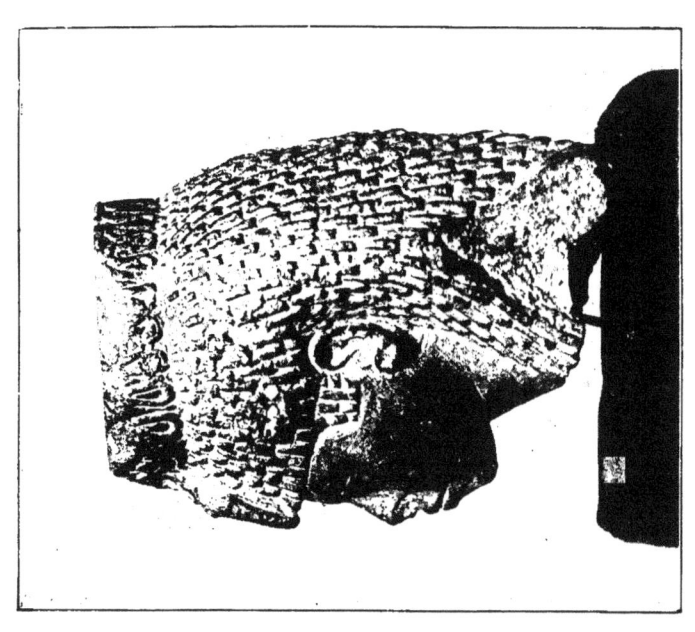

QUEEN TÎYI (PROFILE).
Cairo Museum.

QUEEN TÎYI (FULL FACE).
Cairo Museum.

Four Canopic Heads

the *coufeh* with hanging ends, the bust is bare; in his right hand he holds the hooked staff and the sacred whip emblems of royalty; the left hand is indolently stretched over the thigh. The body is young, the muscling supple and thick, and although he sinks down a little, he has not the squat attitude we know so well. The face and neck are somewhat slender, and contain the characteristics that, exaggerated later, lent themselves almost naturally to caricature. It is, in fact, the effigy of the young king sculptured at Thebes at the time when he was only Amenôphis IV, but when he demanded that he should be represented as he was, or as he saw himself, without reference to the conventional type of the Pharaoh. In the second piece, a statue of which only the head and shoulders remain, he is some years older. He is armed for war, and his neck, too slender, has bent under the weight of the helmet, as if thenceforth incapable of supporting it. It is the profile of the bas-reliefs of El-Amarna with the rounded spine and the particular curve that projects the head forward; the forehead, nose and mouth only differ from those of the statuette in that they are thinner. A plaster mask in the Cairo Museum which Petrie considers to have been moulded on the corpse immediately after the sovereign's death, but which is undoubtedly a studio model, testifies to a condition of physiological degeneracy that did not before exist. It presents the emaciated features of the bas-reliefs and their bony texture, it is true, but without their extreme exaggerations. When it was question of a statue, the sculptor forbade himself the liberties that his colleagues, commissioned to decorate the tombs, allowed themselves with the master: he represented him just as he was at the moment, and the physiognomy was sufficiently original for him to be certain

Studies in Egyptian Art

of always deriving from it a work that would force the attention of the spectators.

And now let us compare each of these pieces with our Canopic heads. The profile of Khouniatonou helmeted is not as strong as theirs, due perhaps to the contusions undergone by the surface of the stone during a long sojourn in a damp soil where saltpetre was abundant, but each of the elements may be superposed and adjusted, forehead, nose, eyes, mouth, chin, in an absolutely satisfying manner: it merely seems that the artist of the Canopic heads saw his model in better health than that of the statue. The resemblance, although less complete, with the statuette of yellow soapstone is still apparent. No unprejudiced observer with the series in front of him can come to any other conclusion than that we have in it portraits of one and the same man. Leaving out the slight differences due to the chisel, there is no more deviation between the group of statues and the best of our heads than there is between that and the three found with it. There is divergence in one point only: in the two statues the head bends and leans forward more or less; in the Canopic jars it is erect without weakness. A moment's reflection will show that it could not be otherwise. However greatly we are moved by the beauty of the work, we must not forget that our four heads belong, not to art pure and simple, but to industrial art, and that their purpose imposed special rules on the master who chiselled them. They were prosaic lids for the receptacles in which the entrails of the Pharaoh were placed, and it was necessary that the median axis of the vase properly so-called should coincide exactly with that of the lid. There was a question of equilibrium to be managed between the two constituent elements of the Canopic jar; the

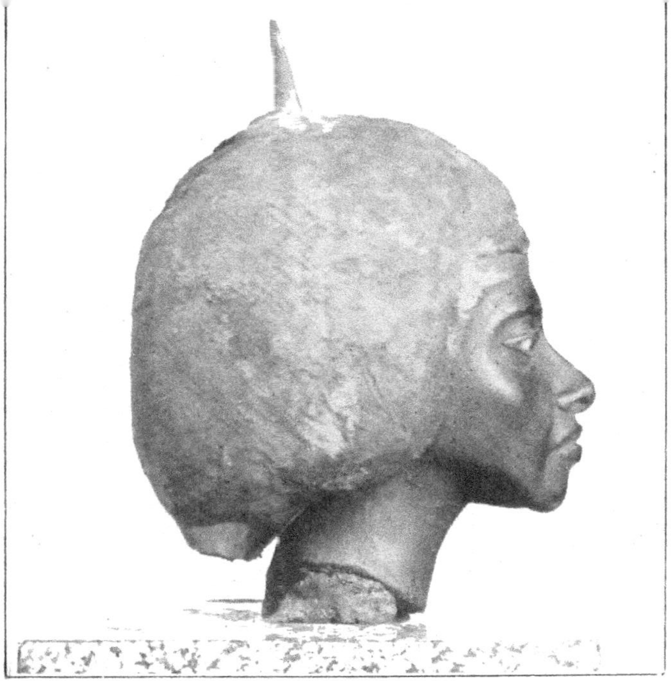

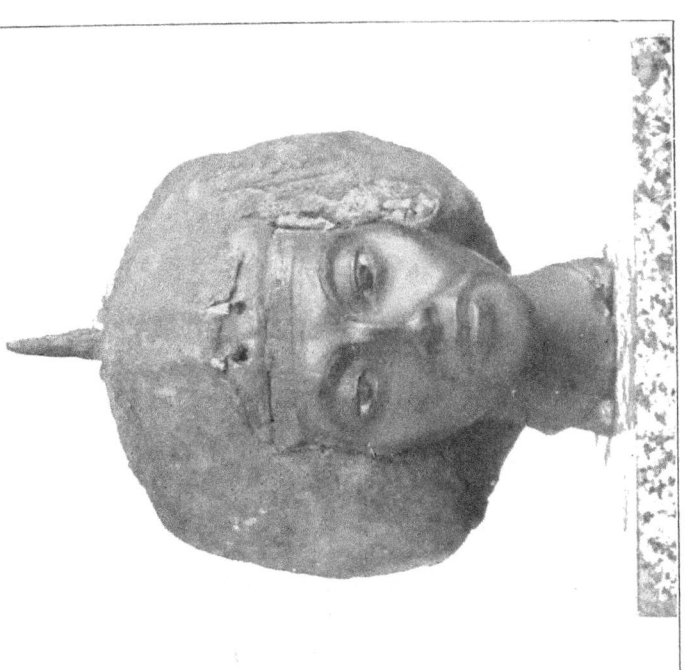

PRINCESS OF THE FAMILY OF TÎYI (PROFILE).

Painted wood. Berlin, collection of M. James Simon.

PRINCESS OF THE FAMILY OF TÎYI (FULL FACE).

Painted wood. Berlin, collection of M. James Simon.

To face p. 132.

KING KHOUNIATONOU.
The Louvre.

Four Canopic Heads

sculptor must straighten the neck of his model, and consequently correct the impression of lassitude given by the statues, by an appearance of vigour. If we examine the portraits of Khouniatonou and his successors in company of a physician, certain anatomical details that at the first glance we did not trouble about—the depression of the temples, the obliquity of the eyes, the contraction of the sides of the nostrils, the pinching of the mouth, the attenuation of the neck—assume an etiological value that the archæologist was far from suspecting. Dr. Baÿ, studying the faces of Khouniatonou, Touatânkhamânou, and Harmhâbi with me, diagnosed symptoms of consumption more or less advanced. If Khouniatonou died of the disease when thirty years old, we need not be greatly surprised.

I do not insist upon this kind of research, in which I am not competent, and I leave it to the reader to decide if I have or have not proved the identity of the person represented by our four heads to be that of Khouniatonou, the heresiarch. One of them at least is a masterpiece, and the others possess qualities that assure them a high place in the estimation of connoisseurs, but to which of the great Egyptian schools ought we to attribute them? We may hesitate between two: the Theban, to which most of the artists who filled the royal laboratories then belonged, and the Hermopolitan, in the province of which was El-Amarna, the favourite residence of the sovereign. It was certainly the latter school that worked at the hypogeums and sculptured the pictures. We find in them its defects: harsh, rough composition, a tendency to caricature the human form and to multiply comic episodes; but also its good qualities: suppleness, movement, life, freedom of execution. The few figures in alto-relievo that have escaped destruction, those, for instance, that aecom-

Studies in Egyptian Art

pany two of the large front stelæ, are of the same style as the bas-reliefs, but we do not find in them any of the characteristics that we have noted as proper to the monuments of the Louvre or to our Canopic jars. Just as the others show an unfinished, worn aspect, these are carefully finished in the least details: it is the perfect chiselling and high polish of the Theban masters and their strong, dignified way of posing the figure and expressing the physiognomy of the model. Whoever has seen the statues of Thoutmôsis III, Amenôthes II, the so-called Taia, and Touatânkhamânou in the Cairo Museum will not doubt for a moment that our four heads are from the hands of persons belonging to the same school: they belong to the Theban school, and more particularly, I think, to that portion of the Theban school which, a few years later, decorated the temple of Gournah, the Memnonium of Abydos, and the hypogeum of Setouî I.

KING KHOUNIATONOU.
Fragment of a stone statue. The Louvre.

XIV

A HEAD OF THE PHARAOH HARMHABI

(*Boulaq Museum*)

THE whole is composed of about ten pieces, collected in 1860 in one of the halls of the temple of Karnak, and put together with plaster, for good or ill, by one of the workmen belonging to the Museum. The cementing was not always done with rigorous accuracy, and one of the largest fragments, that which forms the centre of the head-dress, is slightly out of the perpendicular. Last year I tried to remedy the awkwardness of the restorer, but without success; if an attempt was made to separate the badly joined pieces, there would be a risk of reducing them to powder. But the irregularities in the joining are sufficiently slight not to injure the general aspect. In its present condition it is just the mutilated bust of a king with the uræus and the double crown on the brow; the broken object that leans against the left side is the end of a staff of office, terminated with a ram's head, the emblem of Khnoum or Theban Amon. If we would form some idea of what the body was like, it is sufficient to look at any of the statues with the insignia that adorn the museums, that of Ramses II at Boulaq* or of Setouî I

---

* Mariette, "Notice des principaux monuments du Musée de Boulaq," 6th edition, 1876, p. 300, No. 100 C.

Studies in Egyptian Art

in the Louvre.* The king was standing, with his back against a sort of pillar covered with inscriptions, and holding the staff in his hand: as he looked in certain religious ceremonies when he escorted the ark of Amon-Râ through the halls and court-yards of the temple. What remain of the hieroglyphic legends do not give any name. Mariette was tempted to recognize it as Menephtah, son of Ramses II,† but he has not anywhere explained the motives that led him to that identification. The lugubrious tone of the black granite spoils the first impression, but an examination, even if only a superficial one, soon reveals the subtlety of the work. The head, under the enormous pschent, is full of charm and delicacy. The face is young, with an expression of gentle melancholy rare among the Pharaohs of the great Theban period. The nose is straight, thin, and well attached to the forehead; the long eye turns up at the temples. The wide, full lips, somewhat tightened at the corners as if for smiling, are boldly cut with sharply defined edges. The chin is scarcely rendered heavy by the weight of the artificial beard. Every detail is treated with as much skill as if the sculptor had been manipulating a soft stone like limestone, and not one of the materials that offer all the obstacles possible to the chisel. The sureness of the execution is carried so far that the spectator forgets the difficulty of the work in order to think solely of its intrinsic value. It is a pity that Egyptian artists did not sign their works: the name of the master to whom we owe this deserves to have come down to us.

* E. de Rougé, "Notice sommaire des monuments égyptiens," 3rd edition, 1864, p. 34, A 21. The British Museum possesses a replica of this statue.

† Mariette, "Notice," 1st edition, 1864, p. 184, No. 17; and 6th edition, 1876, p. 92, No. 22.

HEAD OF THE PHARAOH HARMHABI.
Black granite.

The Pharaoh Harmhabi

It remains to see who was the king whose portrait he has transmitted to us. When a Pharaoh ascended the throne, the sculptors of the city where he then was, Memphis, Thebes, Tanis, or another, hastened to make a certain number of copies of his portrait, full face or in profile; these were immediately sent into the provinces, in order that his face might be everywhere substituted for that of the former sovereign on the buildings in course of erection. Thus in the Boulaq Museum we have several series of royal heads, some discovered at Tanis,* some in the Fayoum,† others at Memphis,‡ which show what was the procedure in such a case. The type, once carefully fixed, did not change during the whole of the reign. Ramses II, who was nearly a hundred years old when he died, after reigning for sixty-seven years, kept the features of a young man even to his latest monuments. The rule contains numerous exceptions, especially when it is a question of statues commissioned in one of the capitals of the country, and executed by artists who could see their subject at close quarters and register the changes time produced in his face. Of the two Chephrên exhibited at Boulaq, one is young and smiling,§ the other old and saddened by age.‖ But if there are examples of sovereigns who, ascending the throne early, were sometimes represented as they were at different periods of their life, I know of none who were rejuvenated by the sculptors when

---

* Mariette, "Notice," 6th edition, p. 221, Nos. 638-48; Maspero, "Guide du Visiteur au Musée de Boulaq," 1883, pp. 100-3.

† Mariette, "Notice," 6th edition, p. 221, Nos. 649-51; Maspero, "Guide," p. 101.

‡ Mariette, "Notice," 6th edition, p. 221, Nos. 623-37.

§ Mariette, "Notice," 6th edition, pp. 212-13, No. 578; Maspero, "Guide," p. 75, No. 396.

‖ Mariette, "Notice," 6th edition, p. 239, No. 792.

Studies in Egyptian Art

they reached the throne at a late age. The head of the statue with which we are here concerned is that of a young man, almost a youth, and that is sufficient for me to rule out Menephtah. Menephtah was fifty at least when he succeeded his father,* and his portrait, as it is to be seen at Karnak, does not in any way resemble the personage whose image is preserved in the Boulaq statue. The other princes of the XIXth and XXth Dynasties, Setouî II, Siphtah Menephtah, Amenmeses, Setinakht, of whom we have only a few poor portraits, have no more claim to be commended than their great predecessors Setouî I or Ramses II: the disturbed times in which they lived scarcely admitted of works of careful composition. Like Menephtah, Ramses I was too old at his accession, and besides, we have his portrait at Gournah. And, moreover, the style of the piece recalls at first sight that of the Turin statues belonging to the XVIIIth Dynasty, and then we must eliminate *a priori* a certain number of statues of which we possess the exact description. Neither Ahmôsis I, nor the Thouthmôsis, nor the Amenhotpou have anything in common with our personage; and for even a stronger reason we cannot recognize in him the characteristic physiognomy of Khounaton and Aï. Proceeding from one exclusion to another, we come to restrict the choice to three princes, Touatânkhâmonou, Sânakht, and Harmhabi. Sânakht had only an ephemeral reign; Touatânkhâmonou has only left us insignificant monuments; Harmhabi, on the contrary, appears to have been one of the most important sovereigns of his time. A young man

---

* Maspero, "Letter to M. Gustave d'Eichtal on the circumstances of the history of Egypt which favoured the exodus of the Hebrew nation," in the *Comptes Rendus de l'Académie des Inscriptions et Belles-Lettres*, 1873, pp. 37–8.

The Pharaoh Harmhabi

at the accession, he restored the temples of Amon despoiled by his heretic predecessors, and re-established the Egyptian power that had been weakened for a moment in Syria and Ethiopia. Last year and this year I cleared away the rubbish from two of the pylons he had built and decorated at Karnak; his portrait was sculptured on them numerous times, and the outlines are sufficiently well preserved for us to see in the king of the bas-reliefs the original of the Boulaq bust. I attribute the statue of which Mariette found the remains to Harmhabi, the Armaïs of the Greeks.

In conclusion, I may observe that the fragments, when carefully examined, show no trace of having been broken by a hammer; the statue was not destroyed by the hand of man, the case with a certain number of the monuments at Karnak. The great earthquake of the year 27 B.C., which put the temple of Amon almost into the condition in which we see it, brought down the ceilings of the halls; all the objects underneath were injured by the blocks or architraves then violently thrown to the ground and crushed under the weight of the ruins. Our Harmhabi did not escape the common lot: it needed Mariette's great patience to restore the little we possess of him.

XV

THE COLOSSUS OF RAMSES II AT BEDRECHEÎN*

RAMSES II, Sesostris, having restored the portions of the great temple of Phtah at Memphis, which bordered the sacred lake on the west and south, had colossi erected in front of the doors, destined to perpetuate his memory and his features for all "who should come after him on the earth, priests, magicians, scribes," and who should recite a prayer to the gods on his behalf. The sacristans appointed as guides to the profane, and the dragomans who act as showmen of the wonders of Egypt, never fail to draw the tourist's attention to these statues; it gives them an opportunity to relate some amusing story like those collected by Herodotus and transmitted to us by him as authentic history. One day Darius I wished to consecrate his image in the neighbourhood, but the high priest opposed his purpose: "Sesostris," he said, "has conquered all the nations that obey you, and the Scythians to boot, on whom you never succeeded in inflicting much harm. There is then no reason why your monument should be placed by the side of that of a Pharaoh whom you have neither surpassed nor equalled!" When Memphis fell and became Christian, the fame of the colossi died away. When it perished and its temple of Phtah was dismantled

* Published in *La Nature*, 1892, vol. lix., pp. 161–3.

THE HALF-BURIED COLOSSUS OF RAMSES II.

THE COLOSSUS OF RAMSES II EMERGING FROM THE EARTH.

The Colossus of Ramses II

stone by stone to serve for the building of Cairo, they were thrown down, and for the most part cut up into grindstones, whence they passed into the lime-kiln. One of them, however, thrown from its pedestal and lying face downwards on the ground, was covered with rubbish, and preserved from destruction by that happy chance. Brought to light by Caviglia at the beginning of the nineteenth century, it had the good luck to please travellers, and owed it to them to have escaped the mania for destruction that possesses the fellahs.

All Europeans in turn who have visited Egypt have admired it. It lies along the side of the path under the palm-trees of Bedrecheîn at the bottom of a muddy ditch. At the period of the inundation, water fills it and covers the statue for some weeks; then it gradually reappears, the shoulder and the leg first, then the bust and face, until it is all high and dry again in its hole. Its Pharaoh was standing, walking, the arms close against the sides. The name of Ramses II is to be read on the cartouche engraved on the buckle of the waistband that fastened his petticoat. Nitre has destroyed one side of the face and body, but what remains suffices to show the excellence of the work. The profile is that of the young Ramses, with low forehead, large aquiline nose, rather a large mouth, and a haughty expression. The base is at some distance off, and farther away still, to the south, a smaller colossus in wood, débris of walls, and fragments of statues point out the position of ancient chambers. The palm forest which flourishes on the site harasses excavation and prevents us from reconstituting the plan. The building or group of buildings that our colossus adorned went along the south bank of the sacred reservoir on which the mysteries of Phtah and the Memphian gods were cele-

Studies in Egyptian Art

brated on the canonical days. In spite of the long period of time, alluvial matter has not succeeded in entirely filling the lake. The place is marked by a noticeable depression, and the earth which fills it, instead of being planted with date-trees, is sown with corn; it is like a square basin the edges of which are drawn downwards from the surrounding ground. The rise of the river partly restores the original aspect of the spot, but the setting of porticoes and pylons which framed it has vanished; it is replaced by clumps of big trees, under which is situated the village of Tell-el-Khanzîr.

It seems that Mohammed-Ali formerly gave Ramses II to England; the fact is not exactly proven, and to admit it definitely a more serious authority than that of one or several of the "Travellers' Guides to Egypt" would be required. The English have not availed themselves of the doubtful tradition to remove the colossus: they were satisfied to set it up again. They did not succeed at the first attempt, and two trials made by Messrs. Garwood and Anderson failed ignominiously enough. General Stephenson, who long commanded the army, was more successful. He first had the ambitious project of setting the statue on its feet again, but as the subscription opened for that purpose did not produce sufficient money, he contented himself with raising it up above the level of the inundation. The operations, conducted by Major Arthur Bagnold, of the Engineers, were begun on January 20, 1887.* Having drawn off the water, he applied eight

---

* Major Arthur Bagnold published an account of them, with three drawings by Wallis and a few sketches, "An account of the manner in which two Colossal Statues of Rameses II at Memphis were raised," in the *Proceedings of the Society of Biblical Archæology*, vol. x., p. 452 *et seq.*

The Colossus of Ramses II

lifting jacks of differing force along the body: the effort was directed alternately to the head and the feet: as soon as the whole mass was raised a little more than a foot and a half, huge beams were slipped underneath, and the hollow was filled up with broken potsherds collected in the ruins of the ancient city, reduced to tiny pieces and beaten so as to form a compact bed. The work was finished on April 16th. The colossus now lies on its back, the face to the sky. A pent-house shelters the head; a thick brick wall surrounds it and protects it from the gaze of the inquisitive crowd. Its guardian dwells beside it in a small two-roomed house where Major Bagnold installed him, and he only shows it to visitors on payment of two Egyptian piastres: it costs about sixpence to see it at the bottom of the new funnel in which it is plunged. The "Service des Antiquités" employs a portion of the tax in keeping it in good condition. Another Ramses in granite and a stele of Apries found in the neighbourhood were afterwards placed there, and complete the little open air museum.

The Arabs call the colossus *Abou'l-Hol*, the father of the Terror, like the great Sphinx. I do not know what they think now that it is under lock and key in its enclosure, but they were really frightened of it when it was, so to speak, at large. The ancient Egyptians believed that statues, human and divine, were animated by a spirit, a *double*, detached from the soul of the person they represented. The *double* ate, drank, even spoke at need, and pronounced oracles; it has survived the religion and civilization of the ancient people, but the changes that have taken place around it seem to have soured its character. It plays evil tricks on those who appproach its hiding-place, injures them, at need even kills

Studies in Egyptian Art

them: Arab writers have a thousand tales of persons who suffered because they imprudently attacked a monument and the spirit that guards it, The means of rendering the *Afrite* powerless is to destroy, if not the whole statue, at least its face: that is why so many Pharaohs have their noses broken or faces damaged. The spirit of Ramses II walked in the palm forest at night, and it was therefore imprudent to venture in the vicinity at twilight. Every time that I was obliged to go that way at sunset, my donkey-boy mumbled prayers and urged on his beast. One evening when I asked him if he was afraid of some *Afrite*, he entreated me to keep silence, assuring me that it was ill to speak of such things, and · that if I persisted some accident would happen to me. In fact, my donkey stumbled in the middle of the forest and threw me against the trunk of a palm-tree: if the donkey-boy had not caught me and averted the blow, I should have smashed my head. From that time, whenever there was talk of the danger in speaking disrespectfully of the spirit that lives in the statue, what had happened to me was always quoted. The whole of Egypt is full of analogous superstitions, the greater number of which are derived from the ancient beliefs, and have been transmitted from generation to generation, from the time of the Pharaohs, the builders of the Pyramids.*

* I have related many examples of this belief in spirits inhabiting the ancient monuments in "Egypt: Ancient Sites and Modern Scenes," 1910, chap. xv., p. 155. I have collected many more, and hope one day to have an opportunity of publishing them.

XVI

EGYPTIAN JEWELLERY IN THE LOUVRE *

So much has appeared in the newspapers about the treasure unearthed at Dahchour last year by M. de Morgan, that every one in Europe knows the number, form, and richness of the objects it comprises; but among those who have described and justly praised them, how many —I do not say Englishmen or Germans, but Frenchmen alone—know that the Louvre possesses a collection of the finest Egyptian jewellery? Mariette was fortunate enough twice in his life to find a number of magnificent ornaments of great artistic value on the royal mummies, at the Serapeum in the tomb of the Apis buried in the reign of Ramses II by the care of one of the sons of the conqueror, Khâmoîsît, high-priest of Phtah, and regent of the kingdom for his father, and at Thebes in the coffin of a queen of the XVIIIth Dynasty, Ahhotpou I, who in her lifetime was the daughter, sister, wife, and mother of Pharaohs. Mariette, artist as he was, very skilfully brought out the interest of his discovery, and the admirable idea it gave of the goldsmiths of the seventeenth and fourteenth centuries B.C., but he went no further. He had brought to light so many monuments of importance for the study of

* Published in *La Nature*, 1894, vol. lxiii., pp. 230–4.

Studies in Egyptian Art

political history and of civilization, that he never had time to dwell much on the secondary result of his works. The jewellery of Ahhotpou is preserved in the Boulaq Museum, where thousands of tourists admire it every winter; that of the Serapeum is placed in the Louvre, and usually obtains only an absent-minded glance from the few visitors who traverse the solitudes of the Charles X Museum.

It fills several compartments of a glass case that stands in the centre of the historic hall. At first we note a large gold mask, unfortunately damaged, and grouped near it gold chains with five and eight strands of extraordinary suppleness and perfection; amulets of various shapes in felspar, red and green jasper, and cornelian; scarabs, a buckle, an olive, a little column, in the name of Khâmoîsît. A little farther on a second series from the same source includes pieces, if not in themselves more finished, more curious and more attractive to a modern eye; the Lord Psarou, who was present with the prince at the funeral of an Apis, did honour to the mummy of the sacred bull. I imagine that the greater number of our contemporaries have but vague notions regarding the way in which the Egyptians wore jewels. Men or women, their costume at first was summary enough : the men protected their loins with a cloth which scarcely reached the knee and left the bust entirely bare; the women crept inside a clinging smock which reached the ankle, went up to the pit of the stomach, disclosed the breast, and was kept in place by two straps over the shoulders. Jewellery served partly to hide what the stuff left uncovered, at least with the women. A necklace of several rows encircled the neck and came down to the rise of the breasts; large rings

EGYPTIAN JEWELLERY OF THE XIXTH DYNASTY.
The Louvre.

GOLD PECTORAL INLAID WITH ENAMEL.

Egyptian Jewellery

were round the wrists, the upper part of the arm, and the lower part of the leg. The hair, or rather the wig, clothed the back and half the shoulder; a square plaque suspended by a chain of beads or a leather strap hung down below the necklace into the space between the two breasts. That is what we call the pectoral. It often looks like the façade of a temple, surrounded by a torus, and surmounted by a curved cornice; portraits of gods or sacred emblems were crowded on the surface, and inscriptions scattered everywhere tell us the name of the owner, accompanied generally by pious formulas.

The buckle of Psarou must have served to fasten the linen waistband which confined the loin-cloth, or the band which went round the head and kept the head-dress in place. His pectoral is one of the richest that has come down to us. It is fashioned in a plaque of green basalt, polished and sculptured with a precision that is astonishing when we remember how imperfect were the tools at the disposal of the Egyptians. The central scarab is in very high relief against the flat background, and the fidelity of the modelling is marvellous: the smallest details of the head and corslet are rendered with almost scientific truth. The two women who seem to worship it on the right and left are Isis and Nephthys, the two sisters of Osiris. The contours of their bodies are cut in the gold leaf that frames the scarab. Another pectoral of which I give a reproduction is of less delicate workmanship, but the technique presents interesting peculiarities. It has openings cut in it, and the design of the parts is obtained by partitions of a very supple gold, in which are set the scarab and the coloured glass which relieve the uprights and cornice of the naos. The

Studies in Egyptian Art

scarab is in lapis lazuli, the dress of the goddesses in brilliant gold, engine-turned to simulate the stripes of the stuff. The mystical meaning of this design would not escape any educated Egyptian. The scarab represents the heart and life of man, where life resides; it is the amulet which ensures to each man, living or dead, the ownership of his heart. That is why it was given to wealthy mummies, if not to all mummies: sometimes it was stuck on to the skin of the corpse with bitumen at the rise of the neck; sometimes it was set in the centre of a pectoral, lost in the thickness of the swathings over the chest. As every Egyptian, when he left this world, was assimilated to Osiris and became Osiris himself, the heart and the scarab passed as the heart and scarab of Osiris, over which Isis and Nephthys watched, as they had watched over Osiris; hence the figures of the two goddesses. They warmed the heart with their hands, they recited the formulas that prevented it from perishing, they kept off evil spirits and the magicians who might have seized it for their dark purposes. Religion provided the artists with a subtle motive of decoration; while they never went far beyond the primary idea, they varied its detail and expression with much skill. The women are sometimes standing, sometimes seated or kneeling; they extend their arms in front of them, or lift them to their foreheads like mourners, or let them hang down in token of grief; the scarab rests on a boat or a lotus flower or an altar, instead of floating in air, as in the jewel of the Serapeum. Comparative study of all the scenes would prove once again the Egyptians' fertility of imagination and their skill in ringing the changes on the most hackneyed subjects.

The pectoral in the centre belonged to Ramses II

PECTORAL OF RAMSES II.
The Louvre.

PECTORAL IN SHAPE OF A HAWK WITH A RAM'S HEAD.
The Louvre.

Egyptian Jewellery

himself, or, at least, was executed by his order, and as a personal gift in honour of the Apis that was buried: the cartouche name *Ousirmâri* is placed just below the frieze, and serves, so to speak, as a centre for the composition that fills the inside of the frame. There is first a hawk with a ram's head, with spread wings which curve in order to frame the cartouche: in his claws he holds the seal, the emblem of eternity. Lower, a large uræus and a vulture spread their wings and enfold both the hawk and the cartouche in mutual protection. Two *Tats* symbolize eternity, and fill up the empty spaces in the decoration in the two lower corners. The hawk with the ram's head represents the soul of the sun, the uræus and the vulture are the patron deities of the South and the North: together they defend throughout the whole universe the king whose name stands between their wings, and, by the intermediary of the king, the dead man whose mummy wears the jewel.

Here again the figures are designed in panels of gold encrusted with coloured pastes or small pieces of cut stones. The whole is rich, elegant, harmonious. The three principal motives grow in proportion as they descend to the lower part of the picture, according to an admirably calculated progression. The cartouche with its dull gold occupies the centre; below it the hawk forms a first band of iridescent tones, the lines of which, slightly curved back, correct the stiffness of the long sides of the cartouche; the uræus and vulture, one pair of wings seems to serve for both, envelop the hawk and the cartouche in a semicircle of enamels, the tones of which pass from red and green to dark blue, with a boldness and a feeling for colour that does honour to the taste of the workman. If the general aspect makes an impression of

Studies in Egyptian Art

heaviness, it is not his fault; the form of the jewel imposed by religious tradition is so rigid in itself that no combination can correct the effect beyond a certain point. The rectangular or square frame, the cornice at the top, the two rams' heads which fit in below the cornice, form a squat and massive whole. To fill the interior suitably, it is impossible to avoid adding to the heaviness; in manipulating the empty spaces a slender and narrow appearance is procured, as in one at least of the pectorals of Dahchour. The type of the jewels has its origin in the same ideas or notions whence Egyptian architecture and sculpture are derived: it is monumental, and seems to have been conceived for the use of gigantic beings. The usual dimensions of the pectoral are too enormous for the adornment of ordinary men and women. They only come into their own on the breasts of the Theban colossi: the immensity of the stone body on which their image is sculptured lightens them and seems to bring out their exact proportions.

Sometimes the Egyptians left aside the square form bequeathed to them by their ancestors; the sacred bird left his cage when he could. Mariette found two of these simplified pectorals at the Serapeum, both of which represent a hawk: the first has its ordinary head and bends its wings back, the other has assumed the ram's head and keeps its wings straight. It has the same wealth and the same elegance of line as in the other objects of similar source, but the motive, rid of the enamelled frame in which it was stifled, possesses more charm and is better suited to humanity. The execution is wonderful, and the ram's head, in particular, surpasses in suppleness of workmanship all that is so far known. It is cut in a little ingot of pure gold, but it is not the material that is of most value: the

Egyptian Jewellery

old chaser knew how to model it broadly, and has given it as faithful an expression as if he had cut it life-size in a block of granite or limestone. It is no longer, as everywhere else, industrial art: it is art pure and simple. Mariette, and he understood, considered that he had never come across anything approaching this among the Egyptian jewellery he had seen. The gold ring also belongs to Ramses II. The two little horses who prance on the bezel were celebrated in history. They were called *Nourit* and *Anaïtis-contented*, and were harnessed to the royal chariot on the day of the battle of Qodshou, when Ramses II charged in person the Khitas who had surprised him. The Pharaoh remembered the service they rendered him on that memorable occasion. The chiselling, although not so good as that of the hawk with the ram's head, is very fine: it reproduces very boldly the particular attributes of Egyptian horses, their exaggerated mane, rather thin body, slightly swollen extremities. It is true that the rings, as a rule, are not adorned with subjects in such strong relief: the bezel is composed of a scarab or a metal cartouche turning on a pivot, sometimes engraved with the name of the wearer of the jewel, but more often with a pious formula or a series of symbols of obscure meaning by way of inscription. The larger number of the rings we see in the museums belonged to mummies, and are amulets that give the dead man some sort of power over the inhabitants of the other world: a small number only were used by their owners in their lifetime. They are seals, affixed to deeds like our stamps, just as we affix our signature. They are in every material: gold, electron, silver, bronze, copper, enamel, even in wood, according to the wealth of the individual; some are veritable masterpieces of engraving, but many possess no

Studies in Egyptian Art

more artistic value than the common copper seals bought ready prepared at our stationers'.

The largest of these jewels passed through so many hands before reaching the Louvre that they have sensibly suffered: the panels are warped or even broken, the enamels or encrusted plaques are here and there worn off. The Dahchour jewellery, coming direct from the excavation, has preserved an appearance of freshness which has not a little contributed to increase the admiration of the public: the objects seem scarcely to have left the hands of the goldsmith who fashioned them, and the surprise we experience in finding them still so fresh after more than four thousand years renders us indulgent towards the imperfections that a close examination soon reveals. Their extreme antiquity, and quite rightly, counts for much in the appreciation they receive. It is indeed strange to confirm that from the twenty-fifth century B.C. the Egyptians had carried the technique of precious metals and the art of making jewellery to a very high degree of perfection. This was, of course, already known, for it is not infrequent to find rings, fragments of necklaces, isolated pectorals, some of which perhaps go back to the Ancient Empire, while others belong to the Roman period or betray Byzantine influence: our museums possess them by tens, and there is scarcely a private collection that has not a certain number of them. But these isolated objects do not attract the attention of the public; to rouse its curiosity it is necessary that some happy chance should bring to light a considerable treasure in which specimens of all the types usually collected piece by piece are placed together. Fortunately, these finds are not so rare as might be imagined: if Gizeh can boast of possessing the substance of Dahchour and the queen Ahhotpou, the Berlin Museum has the admirable orna-

Egyptian Jewellery

ments that Ferlini obtained from one of the Ethiopian pyramids; the Leyden Museum and the British Museum shared the spoils of one of the Antouf kings of the XIth Dynasty; and the Louvre carefully preserves the jewels of the Serapeum, the most beautiful of all.

XVII

THE TREASURE OF ZAGAZIG *

I

ONCE more chance has served us well. Workmen who were making a railway embankment on the site of ancient Bubastis discovered, on September 22, 1906, a real treasure of jewellery and Egyptian goldsmiths' work in the ruins of a brick house. They hoped to profit by the find themselves, but one of our watchmen had seen them; he took no action, however, at the moment, for fear of being ill-treated: the next day he reported the matter to the native inspector, Mohammed Effendi Chabân, who at once put the police on their track and informed his chief, Mr. Edgar, inspector-general of the antiquities in the provinces of the delta. Investigations were made in likely places, while the police searched the workmen's houses and recovered some of the pieces that had been carried off. Several that escaped them fell later into the hands of a dealer in Cairo: a gold strainer, three undecorated silver phials, a large chased gold ring which strengthened the neck of a silver vase, fragments of silver cups, all, except the gold ring, of no artistic value. The

* Extract from the *Revue de l'Art ancien et moderne*, 1908, vol. xxiii., pp. 401–12, and vol. xxiv., pp. 29–38.

The Treasure of Zagazig

two most valuable, a silver vase with a goat in gold as handle and a gold goblet in the form of a half-opened lotus, were seized at the house of the fellahs, Moursi Hassaneîn and Es-Sayed Eid, before they had sold them to a local Greek *bakal*. He immediately claimed them of us as his personal property that, failing our unfortunate interference, he would have acquired for ready money. As no reply was vouchsafed to his summons, he went to law with us. The affair dragged on for some weeks, during which Mr. Edgar had the railway works carefully watched. At last, on October 17th, a workman with a blow of his pick-axe laid bare several fragments of silver vases: he tried to conceal them, but our *ghafirs* prevented him, and the search proceeded under the protection of the police: the objects lay in a heap, gold between two layers of silver; the same evening they were in safety. The work was carried out so quickly that nothing was lost, and there was no reason for any one to contest our right to the windfall. To bring this story to an end, I may add that on November 4th the court of Zagazig found the two fellahs guilty of theft, and condemned them to imprisonment and to pay half the costs. But the *bakal* still persisted in his claim, and rumour soon spread among the natives that he had gained his suit in the Court of Appeal: we had been forced to deliver up to him the objects of the litigation under penalty of a considerable fine for each day of delay. The dealers never hesitate to spread lies of this sort among the people: they thereby enhance their prestige with the fellahs, and uphold them in the notion that they have nothing to fear from the " Service des Antiquités."

The treasure safe, we had to take note of the condition in which it reached us. At the first glance, two very

Studies in Egyptian Art

different series were perceived: one, which comprised the jewellery and the gold or silver vases of most skilful workmanship, went back to the XIXth Dynasty; the other was composed exclusively of silver plate, the coarseness of which betrayed a much more recent period. Although it was all found at two separate times, and in two places somewhat distant from each other, did it originally form one collection? As we have seen, the whole made a heap among the débris of two or three jars which were themselves broken in the course of centuries under the continuous pressure of the earth; the objects seemed to have been heaped up irregularly, the most valuable in the middle, the others forming a bed above and below. We had even still adhering to a large fragment of pottery a stem partly of hardened mud and partly of metal, in which we recognized on a precipitate of less ancient earrings and bracelets, the remains of several Pharaonic goblets. How can it be explained that relics of such different epochs should be found in the same place? Many of them are intact, but others have purposely been clipped or broken, and the fragments melted down; they are also mixed with plates of pliant silver and with ingots coming from goldsmiths' workshops like those that still exist. We know what happens not only in Egypt but in European countries when peasants dig up treasure while ploughing their land: they take it to a jeweller, who buys it of them by weight, throws it into the melting-pot, scarcely ever troubling about the loss thus caused to art or science, and transforms it into modern horrors. It is to some adventure of the sort that we owe the possession of our find. A fellah who lived, I imagine, during the time of the Roman domination, found in the ruins near Zagazig, if not at Zagazig itself, silver objects which he

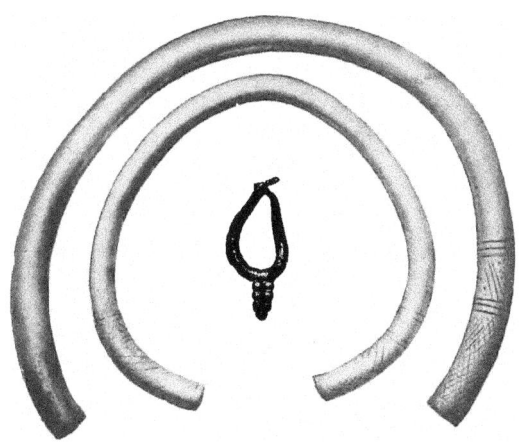

SILVER BRACELETS AND EARRING.

GOLD EARRING FROM THE TREASURE OF ZAGAZIG.

The Treasure of Zagazig

sold to a native goldsmith who destroyed some of them for the needs of his craft, and kept the others either to give to a collector or to use himself in the same way as the first lot when that should be exhausted. Did local sedition or the sack of the city by a hostile army compel him to hide his property in two different places? His goods, once hidden under the earth, were not again drawn forth, and we received them from him, almost without an intermediary, sixteen months ago.

II

I will say nothing of the rubbish of his own fabrication. The types are already those of present-day Egypt, and we could easily swear that most of them were manufactured for sale to the fellahs, at most, twenty years ago : earrings in the form of pendants or oblong rings, to the lower part of which eight or ten metal beads are soldered in bunches ; rings with flat bezels, ornamented or left plain for a name to be engraved ; bracelets formed of a simple reed of silver foil, thinned at each end and covered with a network of lozenges fixed by two or three marks hollowed out by the chisel and lacking elegance, the ends, cut off straight, nearly meet when the piece is finished, but they do not join, and so facilitate the putting of the bracelet on the wrist. It is the honest work of a man who did not spare his material, but only knew just enough of his craft to please easily satisfied customers ; the taste of the good people of Bubastis who bought these things was not of a discriminating sort, or they may have found their market only in the people's quarters. There are much better things of the kind in the Cairo Museum, and if the new-found treasure had only yielded such objects,

Studies in Egyptian Art

it would have been at once despatched to the *salle de vente* for the delight of tourists.

The contrast is striking as soon as we pass to what comes down from the Pharaonic age. Not that it can be placed among the best we know in that kind. The age of Ramses II is already marked by a less sure taste than that of the ages that preceded it, and I cannot compare it with the Dahchour objects nor with those of Queen Ahhotpou. One of the necklaces is the common breastplate of five rows of little tubes in stone and enamel, decorated with a fringe of gold egg-shaped ornaments encrusted with coloured stone. Another necklace, also of gold, with its eight rows of bottle-shaped pendants hanging to little chains of tiny beads, would be somewhat out of keeping with the others if that was its original form, but the parts had been separated, and we remounted them ourselves in order to preserve them with less risk of loss. Five lenticular earrings are formed of two convex gold pellicles closed at the circumference and joined by a border of filigree, stamped in the centre with a rosette, the leaves of which are grouped round a gold or enamel button; a gold tube soldered to the inside and grooved in the furrow of a screw passed through the lobe, and was fastened to an invisible button which, pressed against the flesh, kept the jewel in its place. There was also a bracelet in minute particles of metal and enamel, like those of Ahhotpou and the princesses of Dahchour, but only the clasp has come down to us, a sliding clasp of a most primitive character, with no value except for the gold. The best thing in the series was undoubtedly the pair of gold and lapis lazuli bracelets on which may be read the cartouche name Ousimares—Osymandyas—of Ramses II.

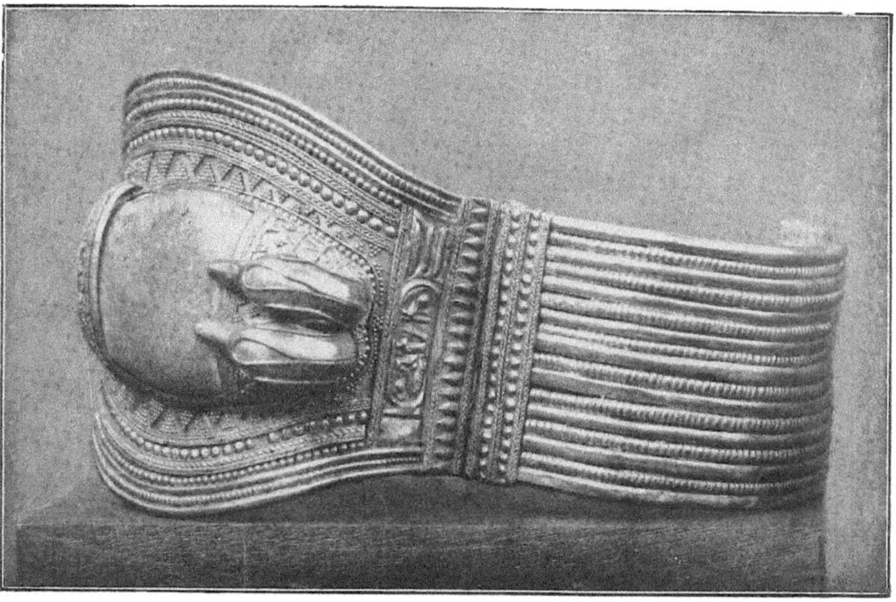

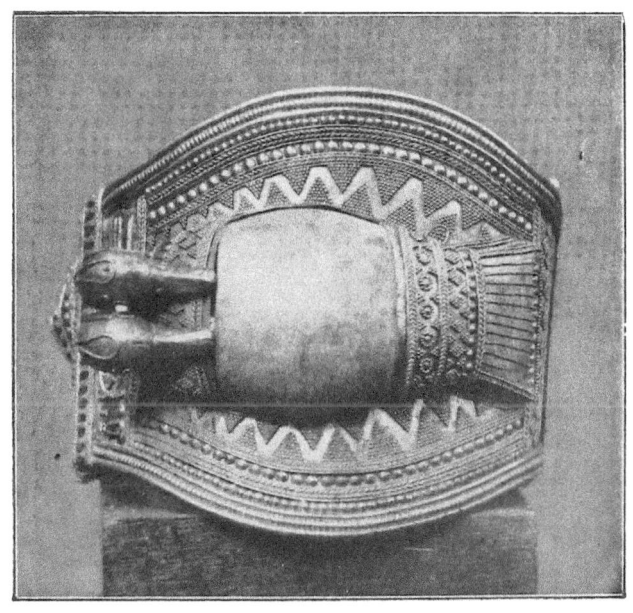

ONE OF RAMSES II'S BRACELETS (OPEN).

ONE OF RAMSES II'S BRACELETS (CLOSED).

The Treasure of Zagazig

They form two circular portions of nearly equal size, joined by two hinges, the first turning on a fixed axis, the second a movable bolt taken away when the bracelet was opened. The back part is a mere plate of polished gold about $1\frac{1}{2}$ inches broad, on which eight twists and eight fillets are laid side by side. The twists and fillets alternate, and the ends are bordered with a thin strip parallel to the hinge. On it are placed two rows of minute particles of metal soldered together, and kept in place by two flat double-twisted little chains. The front portion is expanded to the middle, where it is just over 2 inches in height. At the hinges it is edged by a row of egg-shaped ornaments set between two flat chains, and along the curves by a twist flanked by two fillets. A second frame, included in the first, is of a more complicated design: a double *motif* of little beads and chains goes round the curves, but on the side of the fixed hinge the cartouche name of Ramses II is to be seen, and on the side of the movable hinge two bands of beads and filigree lozenges on a plain background. In the space thus reserved the goldsmith had traced the silhouette of a group of ducks lying flat, by means of a line of beads and a thin thread. The two bodies, which are packed together so as to be combined in one, are formed of a piece of lapis lazuli, cut and highly polished. The ends of the bodies are imprisoned in a gold sheath decorated with a covering of small knobs and lozenges; the tails are joined together, and simulate a fan; they are of lapis, striped with threads of gold to mark the separation of the feathers. Another gold sheath, of similar workmanship, envelops the chest; the two necks escape with a bold movement, and the two heads, twisting round, lie symmetrically on the back of the creatures. Between them and the frame is a smooth ribbon in sharp zigzags on a seed-plot of granules. The

Studies in Egyptian Art

whole effect is rather heavy, and it would have been better if the artist had shown a more sober taste; but having stated so much, it is clearly seen that his work was conceived with a perfect understanding of decoration and a mastery of all the secrets of the art.

All the methods that he so well manipulated may be found in the work of the goldsmiths of contemporary Egypt, especially in that of those who, living in remote villages, have come less under European influence than their colleagues in the cities. The models they copy are never of so delicate an imagination or so skilled an execution; but we note for the most part the same devices and the same decorative parts of which we note the employment here; lozenges, zigzags, simple twisted cords, double-plaited small chains, rounded mallets, threads, filigrees in lines or in seeds. The ingots are beaten, stretched, fashioned, polished on the same little anvil. The granules are blown as formerly in charcoal powder, and the skill with which they are put together and soldered to obtain the desired designs is as great as in the time of the Pharaohs. In that, as in many other industries, the Egypt of to-day has inherited from the Egypt of the past, and we have only to look at the artisans in their shops to learn how the subjects of Ramses II set about their work.

III

The gold and silver vases are some years later than the bracelets. On one of them, indeed, may be read the name of Taouasrît, a great-granddaughter of Ramses II who married successively Siphtah and Setouî II, and who enjoyed her hour of celebrity in the last days of the XIXth Dynasty. It is a half-opened lotus, mounted on

SMALLER OF THE TWO GOLD VASES (FRONT VIEW).

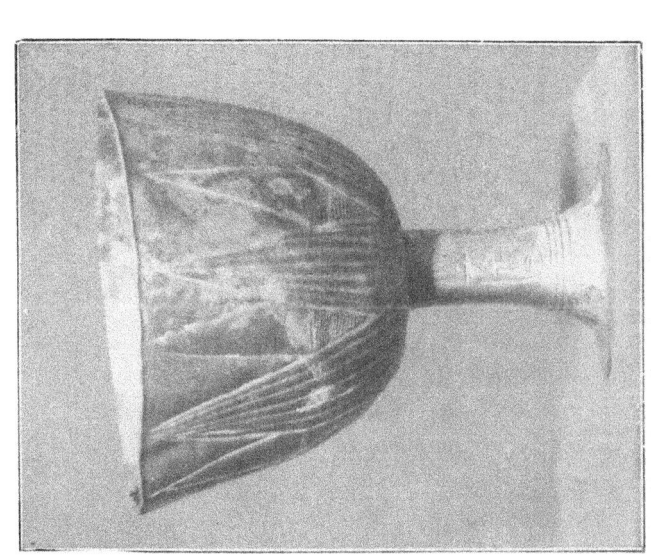

GOLD CUP OF QUEEN TAOUASRIT.

The Treasure of Zagazig

its stem. The calyx of the flower is formed of thin goldleaf, not lined, sharply cut at the outer edge. The stalk is smooth except where the cartouche is engraved: it expands and flattens out at the bottom to form a foot, and the widening is decorated with folioles, kept in place by three circular bands. The lines are sufficiently harmonious, but the execution is poor, and the object would scarcely deserve a brief mention in our catalogue if the royal name did not assign it a definite date: here the artistic yields to the archæological value.

It is otherwise with the gold vases that accompany it. They are of medium size, and the smallest of them all measures only about 3 inches from bottom to top; but the harmony of the proportions makes them perfect models of the kind of plate that appeared at banquets on the sideboards or tables of the rich. The bowl is rounded, and surmounted by a straight neck almost as high as the bowl itself, the upper edge of which curves slightly outwards. The front is decorated with a traced ornament simulating that of one of the large necklaces in lotus petals with which the Egyptians adorned themselves on fête-days. The two bands with which it was fastened to the neck fall undulating on the right and left, and two cats—the two cats of the goddess worshipped at Bubastis—look at them inquisitively, with attentive eye, distended back, quivering tail, straight ears, as if asking to play with them. A lotus escapes below, and on the slopes of its corolla two geese glide flapping their wings. The neck is divided into three equal rows, separated by flat cords: first a wreath of lotus buds points downwards, joined together by a band of threads, one on top of the other; then a row of egg-shaped fruits, and lastly a band of round florets hollowed in the

Studies in Egyptian Art

centre and the hollow encircled with points like stamens. There is neither handle nor holder, but a small barrel, through which a gold ring was passed and by which the object could be hung up, was fastened by three rivets to the lotus buds on the side opposite to that of the necklace. The barrel is of bluish faïence set in a gold mount with a terminal flower. It shows signs of wear and is dented in several places, but none of the blows it suffered have seriously injured it: it is as perfect as at the moment it issued new from the shop. The choice of motives is elegant, the grouping irreproachable, the composition bold and a little summary: the artist seems to have worked quickly, but he possessed such mastery of his craft that the rapidity of the fabrication in no way injured the charm of the work.

The second vase is larger, for it measures about $4\frac{1}{2}$ inches in height; if the shape is similar, the detail of the decoration is very different. The bottom is flat, and the outer surface is filled by a lotus, drawn so as to cover it entirely. The bowl is not smooth, but three-fourths of it are covered with a regular bossage, which gives it the appearance of an enormous symbolic ear of *dourah*. The method employed to produce it is not repoussé work properly so-called, hammered from the inside to the outside. The general network was first very lightly traced on the metal; then the rounds were outlined with a blunt instrument and hammered into a furrow, which, pressing down the metal round them, left them themselves in relief. The neck was finished by an almost imperceptible rim, obtained by turning the upper edge of the gold plaque outwards. There are four rows instead of the three of the small vase: at the top

SMALLER OF THE TWO GOLD VASES (BACK VIEW).

MASS OF SILVER VASES SOLDERED TOGETHER BY OXIDE.

The Treasure of Zagazig

the line of buds, then lotuses head downwards, with alternate bunches of grapes or undefined flowers hanging between them, then centred florets, and then fruits. The suspensory ring is fastened to the band of petals by a *motif* in shape of a calf. The beast lies on its belly, the tail folded over the back; the head, turning to the right, is extended and raised, as if to look over the edge of the neck. It seems to have been chiselled in the solid metal, and not engrafted, and then finished with the graver. It is treated broadly, with a sure touch and the knowledge of animal form that is peculiar to the Egyptians; it may be placed beside the couchant calves that serve as perfume caskets and are masterpieces of sculpture in wood: it will lose nothing by the comparison. The whole presents the same characteristics as the preceding vase, and when closely examined we are soon convinced that it comes from the same workshop; indeed, there is little risk of mistake if we attribute both to the same artist.

It is the same with the two silver jugs which accompany the two gold vases: they have a common origin, and an equal importance for oriental toreumatology. One of them, unfortunately, was broken, and we do not possess all the pieces; but we have enough to be sure that it resembled the one that has come to us intact. The bowl is covered to two-thirds of its height with longitudinal rows of fruits, sitting one on the other like the scales of a pine cone. Here again it is not ordinary repoussé work, but the outline of each scale has been marked round and the metal then pressed down from outside to inside. The smooth belt which lies between the embossing and the rise of the neck carries round the whole of the vase a single line of hieroglyphics ex-

Studies in Egyptian Art

pressing a wish for the eternal life and prosperity of the royal cupbearer, Toumoumtaouneb, then a vignette and the owner in worship before a goddess, who is pacific and Egyptian on the perfect vase, but bellicose and foreign on the broken vase, armed with lance and buckler. Toumoumtaouneb was a person of importance in his time: not only was he entitled chief cupbearer, but he is proclaimed the king's messenger in all barbarous lands, and he doubtless brought back his pious regard for the bellicose goddess from one of his journeys in Syria. That is the only exotic element found in the decoration of the two vases. The top of the neck is ornamented with a rim of light gold. It has two rows of subjects, one on top of the other: episodes of hunting or fishing. A fragment of the broken vase shows a troop of wild horses running towards a marsh with lotuses, where birds are flying. The intact vase is unfortunately encrusted in places with oxide, which obscures the detail of the scenes: we distinguish outlines of boats, tufts of aquatic plants, men drawing nets or shooting arrows, beasts at full gallop; in the upper row there are imaginary trees with palm-leaves or volutes, among which griffins fight with lions. If we do not owe the silver vases to the same artist who fashioned the gold vases, he was at least endowed with the same admirable skill. He has greatly simplified the outline of his figures, but the lines are firm, even, sunk in the metal with the precision of a master: the craft had no secrets from him. But that is not the chief merit of his work: twenty others would have been capable of so much among the goldsmiths who worked for the king and the great nobles. What specially distinguishes it is the originality of the design he chose for the handle, and the manner in which he

LARGER OF THE TWO GOLD VASES (FRONT VIEW).

LARGER OF THE TWO GOLD VASES (BACK VIEW).

THE VASE WITH THE KID.

(About 6¼ inches in height.)

The Treasure of Zagazig

treated it. A kid, attracted by the fumes of the wine contained in the vase, had climbed the bowl, and boldly standing on its hind feet, the legs strained, the spine rigid, the knees leaning against two gold calyxes which spring horizontally from the silver face, the muzzle pressed against the moulding, he looks greedily over the edge : a ring passing through the nostril serves for hanging up the vase. The body is hollow and has been fashioned in two pieces stamped out, and the two halves soldered together longitudinally and touched up with the graver. The horns and ears are inserted : a triangular hole was introduced in the middle of the forehead. The material technique is excellent, but the conception is even superior to the technique : nothing could be truer than the movement that inspires the little creature, nor more ingenious than the expression of greediness emanating from the whole of the body.

Representations of many similar vases may be seen on the monuments of the Theban Dynasties, with foxes, leopards, and human beings for handles, and we had asked ourselves if they really existed anywhere except in the imagination of the painters of the hypogeums. There is now no manner of doubt that they were faithful reproductions of models used by the Egyptians, or by the nations with whom the Egyptians had relations either in war or in commerce. Shall we ever find one of the large table épergnes which show scenes of conquest, with trees, animals, statuettes of negroes or Asiatics in gold or in enamel ? They contained such a large amount of metal that they would have been cast into the melting-pot at some moment of want, but we await the chance that may give us depôts similar to that of Zagazig : I do not think, however, that we shall find pieces of a finer inspira-

Studies in Egyptian Art

tion or of a more harmonious composition than that of the vase with the kid.

IV

The silver wateræ have suffered much. Hurriedly piled up in the receptacle where they were hidden, the oxide bound them solidly together, and we have not yet succeeded in separating them all. It has besides eaten into them in so thorough a fashion that we have only ventured to clean two or three: it is doubtful if we shall ever risk touching the rest. It is a misfortune common to most of the silver objects found in Egypt: under the influence of the annual infiltrations, the organic acids, of which the subsoil of the ancient cities is composed, attack them and eat them away without truce or mercy. If the metal was of suitable thickness we might hope that the surface only was injured and the core of the metal unharmed, but most often they consist of a leaf of metal of extreme thinness, which quickly decomposes. Thus the object only endures at all thanks to the oxide crust, and if that support was removed it would be resolved into dust and tiny fragments.

Only one of the wateræ is almost intact. It measures just over 6 inches in diameter and about $5\frac{1}{2}$ inches in height. It is flat at the bottom and the sides are slightly inflated at the base; they are decorated at the top with a gold border fastened to the rim by rivets. Two small decorated plates in chased gold are furnished with rings which hold a little gold rod that, bent in three, serves to suspend it. Four large gold rounds are placed flat on the rim opposite the handle. The side is smooth, with a single line of hieroglyphics on the outside—a kind wish, on the parvis

ONE OF THE SILVER PATERÆ OF ZAGAZIG (SIDE VIEW).

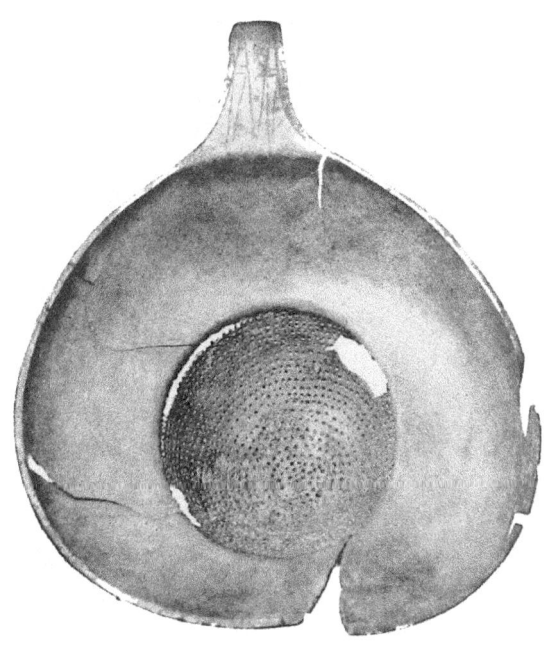

SILVER STRAINER.

The Treasure of Zagazig

of the temple of Neith, for the owner, the singing-girl of Neith, Tamai, "the Cat." It is silver leaf, stamped out in a curve, the two ends of which have been joined without any appreciable overlapping and then soldered together. The bottom is also formed of silver leaf, which is fastened to the lower edge of the sides and divided into two concentric rows. In the centre is a sort of umbilicus, with a gold flat-rimmed hat decorated by a line of rounded beads of metal and several lines of little chains. The row nearest the centre is slightly lower; on it may be seen water full of fish, with tufts of lotus here and there. A little papyrus boat, oceupied by a naked shepherd and a calf, floats amid the patches of green; birds fly about, and two nude figures of young women—the same who, modelled in wood, provided the sculptors of the period with a charming design for perfume ladles—swim side by side in order to gather flowers. A flat space and a line of tiny rounds separate the pool from a hunting-ground that four conventional palm-trees planted at equal distance divide into the same number of distinct compartments. Two winged sphinxes with women's heads stand on either side of one palm, the paw raised and stretched out as if to pull down the dates: two symmetrical pairs of goats leap at the other palms to browse on them. Between these groups, animals run madly about, a wild ox chased by a leopard, hares and gazelles by foxes, dogs, or wolves. The figures of the middle row are of repoussé work of so feeble a character that we should almost say they are engraved on the metal: those of the outer row are of a stronger repoussé, and then gone over again and finished with the graver.

The other pateræ resemble these as far as the technique

Studies in Egyptian Art

and decoration are concerned: they evidently came from the same workshop and belonged to one owner. Were they for daily use or only for ornament? It would seem that they were not fashioned for a definite use: at least they do not recall the shapes seen on the monuments in the hands of guests at a banquet or of priests in the sacrifices. They were hung on the walls of halls, or placed on sideboards on fête-days, and if they were given to the guests, it was not simply for them to eat or drink out of. Filled with fresh water or clear wine, it was a sort of miniature lake, in the centre of which the point of the gold hat rose like an islet: the landscape and figures, seen through the transparent medium, stood out on the flat background with peculiar vivacity, and were effaced or deformed at pleasure when the liquid was disturbed. It is not so long since we were pleased with similar puerilities, and Orientals do not disdain them to-day: the pateræ were, perhaps, toys rather than objects of real utility. I shall not say the same of the silver strainers, the forms of which are elegant but not overladen with ornament, and evidently intended for use. A wide opened funnel, a plaque at the bottom pierced with tiny little holes—the handle alone testifies to any artistic attempt—an open papyrus flower, the petals of which, bent over the stem, lean on the rim of the funnel. It is a useful implement for kitchen or cellar, well adapted to its end, easy to keep clean, in a word practical, a thing in truth that the pateræ are not.

V

It is clear, then, that the interest of the find is great in itself on account of the number and beauty of the

THE BOTTOM OF ONE OF THE ZAGAZIG SILVER PATERÆ.

The Treasure of Zagazig

objects. Until now the greater part of the goldsmiths' work we possess was of the Ptolemaic period, and those that could be attributed with certainty to the Pharaonic period possessed no characteristics that permitted us to judge the skill of the Egyptians. The pictures on the walls of tombs or temples authorize our belief that it was very skilful, but the conventions of their designs are still so ill-defined that there is not always agreement about their interpretation. It is even necessary to ask if certain motives figuring outside a vase ought to be taken as belonging to the decoration of the inside. We now have a sufficient number of their works to justify our con jecture, and to declare in all sincerity that the goldsmiths were in no way inferior to the sculptors, at least so long as the second Theban Empire lasted.

These objects were found on· the site of ancient Bubastis, and the presence of the cats of the goddess Bastit on several of them, as well as the name of Tamai, the Cat, that is on the chief vase, seem to point that they were made in the place that has restored them to us. It is true that Tamai was a singing-girl of Neith, living in the enclosed space before the temple of Neith, and that might be a counter-indication, at least so far as these objects are concerned. Setting aside the question of origin, which is too uncertain, we may ask if they are really Egyptian by inspiration, or if there is not a risk in examining them more closely of the discovery of proofs of some foreign influence. For about a quarter of a century, now, Assyria, Chaldæa, Asia Minor, Crete and the Egyptian islands have become better known to us, and the scholars who have studied those places have not been slow to despoil Egypt in their favour: it is too often sufficient for an object or an artistic design frequently

Studies in Egyptian Art

occurring on Egyptian monuments to be found in those places at once to attribute to them the original invention or ownership. I cannot help thinking that many of these claims are not legitimate, and that in a more general way it is exceedingly rash in the case of a civilization so complex and distant in its beginnings as that of Egypt at the time of the second Theban Empire, to claim the ability to discern all the elements it borrowed from outside. We know how rapidly the peoples of the Nile assimilate the foreigner : in ancient times, it was with the arts as with men, and forms of architecture, of drawing, of industrial production, transplanted among them, either quickly disappeared and left no trace, or yielded to the conditions of the country, and became so completely fused with the taste of its environment that it is now scarcely possible to distinguish the foreign from the native. I believe that Egypt certainly accepted exotic types; but the lands with which she had relations did not abstain from imitating her, and from the most distant ages. She gave to others at least as much as she received from them, and in many cases where the question of filiation has recently been determined against her, it would be well to suspend that judgment, if not to upset it.

In this case, I imagine that it will not enter any one's mind to dispute that the bracelets of Ramses II and the chalice of Taouasrît are Egyptian pure and simple. The two gold vases and the two silver jugs present no foreign characteristic : the gold kid is of the same family as the goats sculptured fifteen or twenty centuries earlier in the Memphian bas-reliefs, standing on their hind legs and nibbling at a bush. The pateræ, it is true, resemble the Phœnician gold and bronze cups so often found in the Euphrates districts and in the lands on the shores

The Treasure of Zagazig

of the Mediterranean: but no one has refused to admit that they were imitations of Egyptian models, and perhaps a more impartial examination would lead archæologists to restore some of them at least to Egypt. At any rate, the treasure of Zagazig shows us what those models ought to be: the Phœnicians were not unmindful of them and respected the general arrangement, even if they often modified the detail. One element only in the scenes of the two rows may be exotic: the female sphinx with the strange locks of hair, if we choose to see in her a derivative of the griffin rather than a fantastic deformation of the male sphinx of a former age. But even so, it must not be forgotten that the griffin belongs to the ancient national foundations like the oxen and gazelles, goats, dogs, leopards seen by its side : its presence would only prove—if its form was so characteristic that we could not refuse to believe it an incongruity—that it was borrowed from the arts of Syria or Chaldæa by some artist tired of always using the traditional types of his country.

XVIII

THREE STATUETTES IN WOOD

(*The Louvre*)

THE three little wooden figures reproduced here are of Theban origin, and represent persons who lived under the conqueror-kings of the XVIIIth and XIXth Dynasties.

The first was found in the Salt collection, purchased by Champollion at Leghorn in 1825, which forms the basis of the Louvre collection.* It is a young woman in a long clinging dress trimmed with a band of embroidery in white thread running from top to bottom. She wears a gold necklace of three rows and gold bracelets. On her head is a wig, the hair of which hangs down to the rise of the breast; the wig is kept in place by a large gilded band simulating a crown of leaves arranged points downwards. The right arm hangs down beside the body, and the hand held an object, probably in metal, which has disappeared; the left arm is folded across the chest, and the hand clasps the stem of a lotus, the bud pointing between the breasts. The body is supple and well-formed,

* Champollion, "Notice descriptive des monuments égyptiens du Musée Charles X," 1827, 8vo, describes the object as follows : "85. *Hard wood.* A woman named Naï, standing, dressed in a long fringed tunic, hair plaited. The statuette was dedicated by her brother, Phtah-Maï, auditor of justice," pp. 68–9. Now the little figure is numbered 37 ; it is in case A of the " Salle civile " (first shelf).

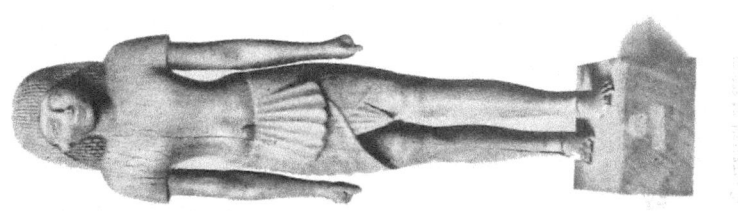
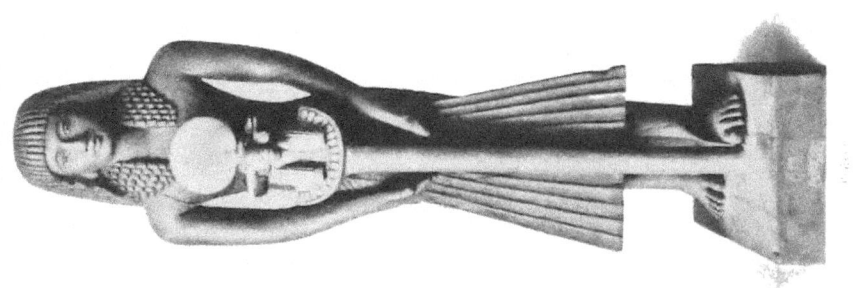

STATUETTES IN WOOD.

Three Statuettes in Wood

the breast young, straight, slight, the face broad, and smiling with something of softness and vulgarity. The artist was unable to avoid heaviness in the arrangement of the coiffure, but he has modelled the body with an elegant and chaste delicacy; the dress follows the form without revealing it indiscreetly, and the gesture with which the young woman presses the flower against her is natural. The statuette is painted dark red, except the eyes and the embroidery, which are white, and the wig, which is black: the bracelets, the necklace, and the bandeau are of a yellow gold identical with the small book exhibited in the glass case marked Z in the "Salle civile." *

Two inscriptions engraved on the pedestal, and then painted yellow, inform us of the name of the woman, and of that of the individual who dedicated the statue. One on the front runs thus:

(A) ADORATION TO PHTAH SOKAR-OSIRI,† GREAT GOD, PRINCE OF ETERNITY, TO WHOM ARE GIVEN ALL KINDS OF GOOD THINGS AND PURE THINGS, TO THE DOUBLE OF THE PERFECT LADY NAÎ OF THE TRUE PERFECT VOICE.

The other is engraved on the right side, and runs:

(B) IT IS HER BROTHER WHO MAKES HER NAME TO LIVE, THE SERVANT PHTAH-MAÎ.

* Cf. E. de Rougé, "Notice des principaux monuments," p. 82.

† SOKARI (Σώχαρις of the fragment of Cratinus the Younger, "Fragm. Comicor. græcorum," edition Didot) was the god of the dead at Memphis, as Osiris was at Abydos; so they were soon identified one with the other, Sokar-Osiri, and with Phtah, *Phtah-Sokari*, *Phtah-Sokar-Osiri*. Here the scribe, who first took the three sacred names as belonging to one same god whom he qualified as Prince of Eternity in the singular, later regarded them as belonging to three different gods, and used the plural pronoun, SE, variant of SEN: "to whom THEY give" instead of "to whom HE gives."

Studies in Egyptian Art

From other monuments we know more than one Egyptian of the name Phtah-Mai, and more than one lady Nai: but none of them has any claim to be identified with our two personages. Phtah-Mai is not a noble: he filled a very humble post, that of a page attached to a noble, or a subordinate employé of a temple or of a court of justice. But the charm of the monument he devoted to the memory of his sister is only the more remarkable.

The personage in the middle is a priest, standing, wearing the short wig with little locks of hair in rows one above the other. The bust is bare, and his only garment is a long skirt falling half way down the leg, spread out in front into a sort of pleated apron. In his two hands he bears a sacred insignia consisting of a ram's head surmounted by the solar disk, and forming an ægis, the whole set into a staff of fairly large dimensions: the attitude is one of repose. The third figure, on the contrary, is full of movement and activity. It is an officer in semi-military costume of the time of Amenôphis III or of his successors: a small wig, a clinging smock with sleeves, a short loin-cloth tightly girded over the hips and scarcely descending to the middle of the thigh, decorated in front with a small piece of stuff standing out, pleated lengthwise. These two statuettes are painted dark red with the exception of the wig, which is black, of the cornea of the eyes, which is white, and the insignia of the priest, which is yellow. The old pedestal has disappeared, and with it the name. Like the limestone and wooden statues of large dimensions, these formed part of the funerary equipment: they were the supports of souls in miniature, and served as a body for the double of the model and *kept alive the name* of a person who had been loved or

Three Statuettes in Wood

well known. There are a large number of them in the museums, and nearly all are of the same epoch. Neither the Ancient nor the Middle Empire made them—Saïte art preferred hard stone: the wooden statuettes that I have so far seen are of the second Theban period, and belong to the XVIIIth, XIXth, and XXth Dynasties.

Some of them, if not all, were used for purposes that seem strange to us. Several had little rolls of papyrus fastened to their pedestal or their body, ordinary letters that the writers sent to one another; one possessed by the Leyden Museum is an adjuration addressed *to the perfect soul of the lady Ankhari* by her still living husband:*
"What fault have I committed against thee that I should be reduced to the miserable condition in which I find myself? What have I done to justify this attack on me, if no fault has been committed against thee? From the time I became thy husband until this day, what have I done against thee that I should conceal? What shall I do when I have to bear witness to my conduct in regard to thee, and shall appear with thee before the tribunal of the dead, addressing myself to the cycle of the infernal gods, and thou wilt be judged after this writing, which is in words uttering my complaint in regard to what thou hast done. What wilt thou do?" The general tone of the piece is, as is clear, one of complaint and accusation. The husband laments about "the miserable condition to which he is reduced," three years after he has become a widower; then he relates the incidents of his conjugal life in order to show the ingratitude he has received for his trouble

* The figure to which it was fastened is reproduced in Leemans, "Egyptian Monuments in the Museum of Antiquities of Holland at Leyden," Part I, Pl. XXIV; cf. Chabas, "Notice sommaire des papyrus égyptiens," p. 19.

and care. "When thou becamest my wife, I was young, I was with thee, I did not desert thee, I caused no grief to thy heart. Now so I acted when I was young; when I was promoted to high dignities by Pharaoh, I did not desert thee; I said: 'Let them be mutual between us!' and as everybody who came saw me with thee, thou didst not receive those whom thou didst not know, for I acted according to thy will. Now, here it is, thou hast not satisfied my heart and I shall plead with thee, and the true will be distinguished from the false." He dwells on and reminds her of his kindnesses: "I have never been found acting brutally to thee like a peasant who enters other people's houses." When she died, during an eight months' absence occasioned by his service with Pharaoh, "I did what was seeming for thee: I lamented thee greatly with my people opposite my dwelling, I gave stuffs and swathings for thy burial, and for that purpose had many linen cloths woven, and I omitted no good offering I could make thee."* The poor man does not state clearly the nature of the troubles from which he suffered. Perhaps he imagined that his wife tormented him in the form of a spectre; perhaps, what after all comes to the same thing in the belief of an Egyptian, he was attacked by diseases and overwhelmed with infirmities that he attributed to the malignity of the dead woman. We are reminded of the strange actions that the Icelanders of the Middle Ages practised against ghosts. The administration set on foot the whole cortège of officials and the whole of its legal code to bring the accusation, judge and condemn the dead who persisted in haunting the house in which they

* The facsimile of the text is in Leemans, "Monuments," Part II, Pl. CLXXXIII–CLXXXIV, and is translated and annotated in Maspero, "Etudes égyptiennes," vol. i., pp. 145–59.

Three Statuettes in Wood

had lived. The records of the causes are extant and testify to the gravity that presided over this strange procedure. The Leyden papyrus certainly relates to an affair of the kind. A husband, addressing his wife's soul, summons her to suspend persecutions that are in no way justified, under pain of answering for her conduct before the infernal jury. If she did not heed this preliminary advice, the matter would be brought later before the tribunal of the gods of the west and pleaded: the papyrus would serve as a piece of convincing evidence, and then "the true would be distinguished from the false."

There was one difficulty to be overcome: how was the summons to be sent to her? The Egyptians were never embarrassed when it was a question of communicating with the other world. The husband read the letter in the tomb, then fastened it to a figure of the woman. Thus she could not fail to receive the adjuration as she received the funerary banquet, or the effect of the prayers that assured her happiness beyond the tomb. The preoccupations of art held only a subordinate place in statues like those of the lady Nai and her two companions: the religious idea was predominant, and it was religion which gave the monument its meaning.

XIX

A FRAGMENT OF A THEBAN STATUETTE *

THE excavations undertaken by Mr. Mond on the eastern slope of the hills of Cheikh-Abd-el-Gournah, in one of the richest of the Theban cemeteries of the XVIIIth and XIXth Dynasties, have already given several valuable monuments to the "Service des Antiquités"; and nothing surpasses or even equals the fragment illustrated here. The statuette to which it belongs was broken in the middle. The hips and legs have disappeared, as well as the right arm, and the plinth against which the back leaned; Mr. Mond eagerly sought the missing pieces among the residue of his find, but in vain; they were not forthcoming, and were doubtless either destroyed in ancient times, or carried off by some amateur during the nineteenth century. The fragment that remains to us measures nearly a foot in length and about $4\frac{1}{2}$ inches across the shoulders; there is nothing in the lines by which one can determine whether the person it represents was seated or standing. I am inclined to think that, according to the custom of the time, the attitude resembled that of the little lady Toui in the Louvre,† standing, the feet nearly on

* Extract from the *Revue de l'art ancien et moderne*, 1905, vol. xvii, p. 403.
† See the Chapter on the little lady Touî, pp. 183–189.

THE MOND STATUETTE (FRONT VIEW).

To face p. 178

Fragment of a Theban Statuette

the same level, the right arm hanging down, the head erect, with the wig of ceremony, and the dress of great holidays.

The material employed by the sculptor is limestone of the kind the inscriptions describe as the *fine white stone of Tourah*, but thick beds of it extend along the sides of the valley of Egypt from the environs of Cairo to the defiles of Gebelein. It abounds in the Theban plain, and although it is too split and cracked in every sense to be of any use for building purposes, it is admirably suited for designs of restricted dimensions, such as those of our statuette. It was most probably carved in the stone of Cheikh-Abd-el-Gournah itself, perhaps in one of the blocks extracted at the time of hollowing out the tomb for which it was destined. It forms an excellent substance, supple and firm at the same time, and subserves with an inimitable docility the boldest and the most delicate strokes of the chisel; the grain of marble, crystalline and almost metallic, makes the sensation on the eye of a rigid envelope in which the subject is, as it were, imprisoned, while limestone, softer and richer, better reproduces the elasticity of the surface of flesh and the free play of the muscles under the skin. Our statuette had been illuminated in accordance with custom, but it bears only imperceptible traces of painting and has the natural colour of old limestone, a tone between cream and yellowed ivory, which recalls the paleness of Egyptian women. The detail of the clothing and ornaments which was due to the brush has vanished, and is only indicated on the border of the mantle by faint tooling. It has thus lost its archæological value, but has gained an aspect of refinement wanting in works where the colour has been preserved intact.

Studies in Egyptian Art

The young woman who has thus left us her portrait lived under the XIXth Dynasty, at a time when fashion imposed enormous head-dresses and scanty clothing on its votaries. An almost transparent linen covers the left shoulder, then crosses the chest and is knotted under the right armpit, concealing the rest of the costume; the left hand is freed from it and clasps a lotus stem, the flower reaching to the hollow between the breasts. The bust has not yet attained its plenitude, but the breasts are well shaped and well separated, but so slight that they scarcely make any impression on the linen; the lines of the arm, shoulder, and neck indicate thinness. The artist has well understood the characteristics of the dawn of womanhood, and the discreet fashion in which he permits us to guess the slender grace beneath the garment is that of a master craftsman, but it is in the head and face that he shows the full measure of his talent. The head is fitted into a wig of complicated structure which yields nothing in size to the majestic peruke of Louis XIV. A double ribbon running from the forehead to the back of the neck divides the hair into two equal masses, which are themselves divided into volutes of little waved locks, each formed of two thin tresses, twisted together at the extremity. The whole forms a stiff heavy fabric which, unskilfully interpreted, would make the piece ugly, no matter how successful in the other parts. Our sculptor has made no change in the general arrangement—his model would not have permitted it—but he has adjusted the parts with such happy ingenuity that the monster wig, instead of overpowering the face, acts as a frame to it and sets it off.

It is of the purest Egyptian type, not the heavy, brutal type which predominates in the Memphian age and

THE MOND STATUETTE (PROFILE).

Fragment of a Theban Statuette

among the fellahs to-day, but an elegant refined type of which numerous examples are provided by statuettes of all periods. The forehead appears to be rather low, but we cannot be sure if it was so by nature, or if it is the wig which conceals its height. The eyes are long, almond-shaped, slanting towards the temple, widely opened. The eyelids are drawn clearly, almost sharply, and meet at an acute angle both at the inner corner and at the outer commissure. The globe of the eye is rather prominent, the pupil was added with the brush, and a sort of greyish tone vaguely marks the place. The eyebrows are a flattened bow, thin and regular. The nose is attached to the superciliary arcade by a fairly accentuated curve; it is straight, thin, rounded at the end, with delicate nostrils. The lower part of the face is thick-set, and of so firm a cut that with age—if age ever came—it would have become hard. The lips are full, thick, edged the whole length, split in the middle: they are pressed together as if to keep back a smile. The whole face changes in character and almost in century, according to the angle from which it is looked at. Seen from the front it is round and full, with neither superabundance nor softness of flesh: it is the little middle-class girl of Thebes, pretty, but common in form and expression. Seen from the side between the hanging pieces of the wig, as if between two long ringlets falling on the shoulders, it assumes a malicious, roguish expression not ordinarily usual in Egyptian women: it might be one of our contemporaries who from caprice or coquetry had put on the ancient coiffure.

Who was she in her lifetime, and what was her name? The fragment which represents her was found at the bottom of a funerary pit, in the court-yard of the tomb

Studies in Egyptian Art

of Menna, and Menna flourished under the XIXth Dynasty. Was she one of his wives, or daughters, or sisters? The inscription which might have told us is heaven knows where, and it will be a great piece of good fortune if it is ever found.

XX

THE LADY TOUÎ OF THE LOUVRE AND EGYPTIAN INDUSTRIAL SCULPTURE IN WOOD *

THE little lady Toui, who entered the Louvre last year, was in her lifetime a singer in the service of Amon. The title gives rise to doubt and scarcely permits us to determine to what class of society she belonged. The singers in the service of Amon were of all ranks, some married, others free. They were all bound to serve the god; they shook before him the sistrum that kept off spirits, or wielded the magic whip, the *monaît*, with which they beat the air to keep off with heavy blows the evil beings who floated invisible in it. The most humble were of easy morals, and the series of licentious vignettes in the Turin Museum leaves no room for doubt regarding the kind of life they led. They were the servants of the temple; they placed their bodies at the free disposal of their master Amon, and whoever addressed them in his name would not meet with refusal. In the Græco-Roman period the high-priest chose a young girl of rare beauty from among the richest and noblest families of Thebes and solemnly dedicated her. She became the chief singer, and shared the life of her companions of lower origin as long as youth lasted; when she was past the age of child-

* Published in *La Nature*, 1895, vol. lii., pp. 211–14.

Studies in Egyptian Art

bearing she retired, and an honourable marriage allowed her to end her days amid the respect of all. The lady Touî's position seems to have been less curious. The wives of priests or those of citizens affiliated to the different brotherhoods of Amon formed associations of *singers* who appeared in the temples on days of festival or at the hours fixed for certain ceremonies: they only accepted the duty of playing the sistrum or of plying the whip, leaving to the others the rest of the function. Toui doubtless had a husband and children somewhere in Thebes. In an Egyptian tale* the heroine, Tbouboui, daughter of a priest of Bastit, replies to the lover who is importuning her: "I am pure, I am no wanton." Toui might say the same to us if, trusting to her title, we confused her with the common *singing-girls*, who yielded their bodies to all.

The statuette that represents her may deservedly rank as one of the best works which have recently emerged from Theban soil. She stands upright in the hieratical attitude of repose, one foot in advance, the head fixed, the right arm hanging by her side, the left arm across the chest, holding the sacred whip, the *monaît*, folded up. She wears the ceremonial costume, a long robe with sleeves, narrow, crossed in front, edged with a heavy, stiff fringe, a broad necklace round the neck; on her head the immense wig fashionable among the Thebans in the eleventh and tenth centuries B.C., numerous little tresses gathered together at the ends into two or three, and finished off with tassels or little curls. The effect was fairly ugly: it lent heaviness to the top of the figure,

* "The Adventure of Satni-Khamois with the Mummies," in G. Maspero, "Les contes populaires de l'Egypte ancienne," 4th edition, p. 146.

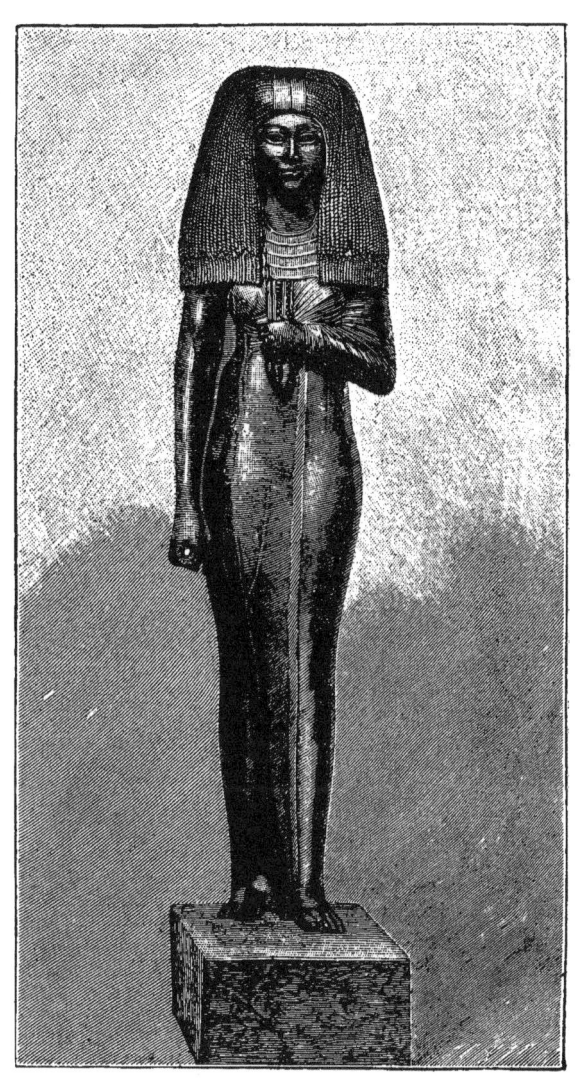

THE LADY TOUÎ, STATUETTE IN WOOD.
The Louvre.

The Lady Toui of the Louvre

diminished the size of the face, cramped the neck, concealed the fall of the shoulders and the rise of the breasts, broke the equilibrium of the body. But the anonymous artist who made the portrait of the lady Toui has derived an almost fortunate advantage from this deplorable headdress: he has treated it as a sort of background which sets off the face, neck, and chest. The lateral tufts of hair frame the features without making them too heavy, and the close-fitting coif at the top is placed on the skull without appearing to crush it. The slender, healthy forms of the body are rendered in remarkable fashion, and the modelling of the belly and legs shows itself under the clinging stuff with a precision that is in no way brutal. In looking at it we certainly recognize more than one defect: the figure lacks suppleness and the face expression; the wood is cut harshly and with an almost puerile detail. The whole, however, pleases by some indescribable simple and chaste charm: the Louvre was perfectly right to acquire it, even if more money was expended than is usual on Egyptian objects of such small size.

Its use is easy to determine; it is a miniature *statue of the double* shut up in the tombs of the Memphian period. A statue was not within the reach of everybody: only the rich could procure one, and people of moderate means were obliged to content themselves with little figures of less cost. The population of priests, *servants*, *singing-girls*, heads of the works who lived round the sanctuary of Amon or in the temples of the necropolis, had many pretensions to luxury with slender resources: their tombs are filled with objects which pretend to be what they are not, and veritably deceive the eye, destined to give the dead the illusion of opulence; massive wooden vases painted to represent alabaster or granite vases, rings

Studies in Egyptian Art

and jewels in glass or enamel that appear to be gold rings and jewels, furniture in common wood, varnished, speckled, veined, to simulate furniture in rare woods. The lady Toui belonged to that half-needy class, and had to substitute statuettes of carved and polished wood for limestone or sandstone statues. All the museums in Europe have similar ones, and through Champollion, the Louvre possessed the lady Naî,* who sustains comparison very well with her new comrade. Egyptian sculptors had acquired veritable mastery in this subordinate form of sculpture, and there are pieces of singular charm among those that have reached us. Take, for instance, the little girl and the woman I have chosen almost at hazard in one of the cases of the Turin Museum. The little girl is standing, one foot in advance, the arms hanging down, naked according to the custom of Egyptian children, with a necklace, and a belt which loosely surrounds the loins, short plaited hair with a tress falling over the ears. The material is less precious than with the lady Toui, and the work less thorough, but has the slim delicacy of a little Egyptian girl of eight or ten years old ever been better expressed? It is an exact portrait, in costume and figure, of the little Nubian girls of the Cataract before the age of puberty obliges them to wear clothes; it is their thin chest, slender hips, clearly cut, delicate thigh, their bearing, hesitating and bold at the same time, the roguish expression of their features.

The other statuette represents a well-developed woman standing on a round pedestal without a scrap of clothing or veil, but very proud of her head-dress, and especially of her big earrings. She touches the right one with her hand

* See pp. 172–174.

STATUETTE IN WOOD.
Turin Museum.

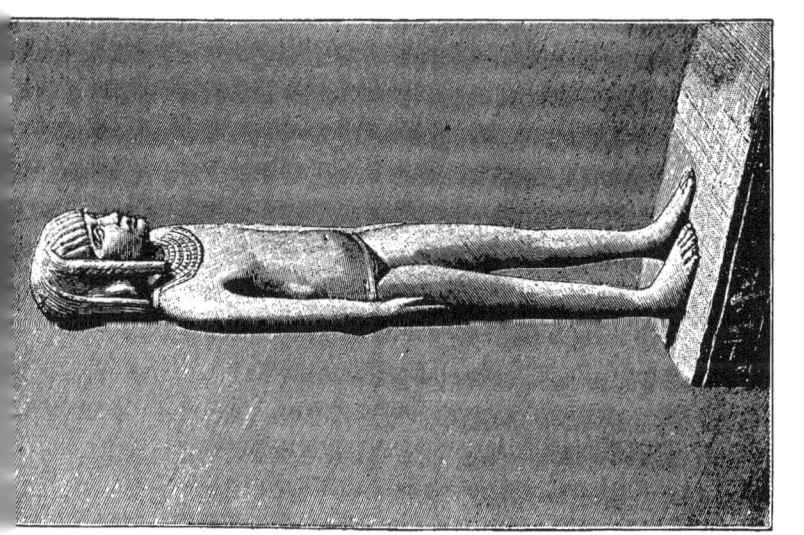

STATUETTE IN WOOD.
Turin Museum.

The Lady Toui of the Louvre

and makes it stand out a little in order to show it, or to assure herself that the jewel is very becoming; the head is big, the shoulders thin, the chest narrow, and the sculptor was embarrassed to render the movement of the arms; but the eyes are so wide open, the smile so contented, the expression of the whole so intelligent, that we can easily excuse that defect.

Men were as well treated as women by this art fostered by persons of small means. Scribes of subordinate rank, old retired officers, retail merchants, or men at the head of small industrial concerns, all of whom swarmed in the poorer quarters, felt as strongly as their wives, in default of the stone statue, the need of acquiring a wooden image which would show what they had been like in their lifetime. There were as many artists as they wished to model them in the attitude they preferred, in their everyday costume or in that of fête-days, bearing and likeness guaranteed. Those found in the tombs in the early years of the nineteenth century form a veritable gallery, most varied and curious, of the different types prevailing from the thirteenth to the ninth century B.C. in Thebes and its environs among the lower middle-class.* Some had been soldiers, and wear the light petticoat bulging at the waist of the Egyptian foot-soldier; others had spent their lives scribbling in a Government office; the greater number belonged to one of the funerary professions, guardians of mummies, decorators of hypogeums, hewers of tombs, sacristans or priests of a low order employed in the minor offices of burials or commemorative rites. They proudly exhibit their insignia: they carry long staves crowned with sacred emblems—the human head of Hathor, the hawk's beak

* See Chapter XVIII, pp. 172–177.

Studies in Egyptian Art

of Horus—and everything in their attitude betrays the pride and satisfaction of knowing themselves so fine and so important. Their bearing reveals what the inscriptions usually placed on the pedestal of their statuettes confirm: "It is I, Khâbokhni, the Servant of the 'True' Place," he who poured the libations, or who, at the canonical hours, distributed a portion of bread, flowers, and fruits to each of the dead entrusted to his care. The Egyptians were admirable in observation and full of satirical humour: I would not swear that, in impressing this character of naïve vanity on their works, the sculptors were not yielding to the temptation of discreetly amusing themselves at the expense of their sitters.

Study of these small monuments is too much neglected. By considering the colossi of granite or sandstone, the heroic statues and the ceremonial groups, we are inclined to recognize only qualities of grandeur and immobile majesty in Egyptian art; the wooden statuettes show how, on occasion, it could display charm and wit. Most of them are the products of chance, commercial pieces, prepared in advance for the needs of customers, of which a large assortment was always kept in reserve. The family desiring to offer one to one of its dead came to get it at the fairest price, and something was sold, more or less well done according to the sum that was spent; the choice being made, the piece was adapted to its definitive destination by engraving on the pedestal, or on the back, the names which transformed the anonymous doll into a body for the double of a particular individual. They were artisans who sculptured these images, or rather manufactured them for the undertakers of funerals. Their education was so complete and their hand so practised that they rarely fell very low;

The Lady Toui of the Louvre

their average productions are of honest composition and sufficiently true in feeling. When they were given enough time or commissioned to take great care with a piece of work, those who combined natural talent with the routine of their craft produced work of real value—the statuettes of the lady Toui, of the little girl and the woman in the Turin Museum, and many others hidden from the public in the cupboards of our museums.

XXI

SOME PERFUME LADLES OF THE XVIIIth DYNASTY

(The Louvre)

IT is not without reason that these objects are called perfume ladles. The Egyptians used them, in fact, for making either essences, pomades, or the various coloured pigments with which both men and women painted the cheeks, lips, eyelids and underneath the eyes, the nails and palms of the hand. The form and decoration vary in accordance with the epochs. At the time of the Ramessides, between the fourteenth and twelfth centuries B.C., fashion introduced Syrian manufactures into Egypt; later, under the Bubastis and under the Ethiopian kings of the XXVth Dynasty, some Chaldæan or Ninevite manufactures came in. The five ladles illustrated here are purely Egyptian in origin and style. The designs were generally borrowed from the fauna and flora of the valley. The first has by way of handle a young girl lost among the lotuses, who is gathering a bud; a tuft of stems from which two full-blown flowers escape attach the handle to the bowl, the oval of which has its rounded part outside and the point inside. In the second, the young girl is framed by two stems of lotus flowers and papyrus, and walks along play-

PERFUME LADLE.

The Louvre.

PERFUME LADLE.

The Louvre.

Perfume Ladles, XVIIIth Dynasty

ing a long-handled guitar. The next ladle substitutes a bearer of offerings for the musician, and the fourth has the musician standing on a boat sailing among the reeds. The last takes the form of a slave, half bent under an enormous sack. Nothing could be better than the general design of the decoration. The artisans brought as much conscience and skill to its execution as the sculptors gave to their colossal statues. The physiognomy and age of the four young girls are well characterized. The girl who plucks the lotuses is an *ingénue*: that state is shown by her carefully plaited hair and her pleated skirt. Theban ladies wore long skirts, and this is only turned up high to facilitate walking among the reeds without soiling its edges. The two musicians, on the contrary, belong to the lower class; one has only a belt round her hips, the other a short petticoat, carelessly fastened. The bearer of offerings has the tress of hair falling over the ear, as was the custom with children, and her belt is her sole garment. She is one of the slender, slim young girls of whom many may be seen among the fellahs on the banks of the Nile, and her nudity does not prevent her from belonging to a respectable family: children of both sexes only began to wear clothes at the age of puberty. Lastly, the slave, with his thick lips, flattened nose, bestial jaw, low forehead, sugar-loaf head, is evidently a caricature of a foreign prisoner; the brutish, conscientious way in which he lifts his heavy burden, the angular prominences of the body, the type of the head, the arrangement of the different parts, remind us of the general aspect of some terra-cotta grotesques that come from Asia Minor.

All the details of nature grouped round and framing

Studies in Egyptian Art

the principal subject, the exact form of the flowers and leaves, the species of the birds, are very accurate, and sometimes betray wit. Of the three ducks that the bearer of offerings has tied by their claws, and which hang over her arm, two are resigned to their fate and go swinging along, the neck stretched out, the eye wide open; the third lifts its head up and flutters its wings. The two waterfowl perched on the lotuses listen at ease, the beaks on their crops, to the lute-player who is passing near them; experience has taught them that they need not disturb themselves for songs, and that a young girl is only to be feared if she is armed. In the bas-reliefs, the sight of a bow or a boomerang throws them into confusion, just as to-day that of a gun scatters the crows. The Egyptians knew the habits of the animals who lived in their land, and took pleasure in minutely observing them. Observation became instinctive with them, and they gave a striking air of reality to the least of their productions.

The bowl of the ladles is generally oval. It is edged by a running decoration between two lines, a waving line, or a more or less accentuated denticulation. The cavity made in the slave's burden is of irregular shape, and the thick border is decorated with lightly carved flowers and foliage. It was a perfume box rather than a ladle, for the little hole in the lower part, near the prisoner's shoulder, held the hinge of the lid, now lost. The fifth ladle is in the shape of a quadrangular trough. The bottom, set in four rectangular mouldings, is covered with waving lines simulating water; the edges represent the banks of the lake and are covered with aquatic scenes. On the right, amid the flowers and lotus buds, a little personage is catching birds with a net; on the left, another is fishing from a boat. They are both summarily indicated, but are

PERFUME LADLE.
The Louvre.

PERFUME LADLE.
The Louvre

To face p 192.

Perfume Ladles, XVIIIth Dynasty

not the less full of life. It is a miniature reproduction on a wooden ladle of the great scenes of fishing and bird-catching which are painted in the tombs and the temples.

The objects are in wonderful preservation. A lid is lost, a lotus branch is broken behind the girl who is gathering flowers, one of the feet of the bearer of offerings is missing. Otherwise they are intact, and might have just come from the hands of the craftsman. The wood is of a very fine grain, marvellously adapted to the needs of the chisel. It has never been painted, but has become darkened with time. The original colour must have been the golden yellow seen in the cracks of some pieces of thin wood found in the tombs. None of the ladles show any signs of wear: they seem to have been deposited new in the tomb near the dead person, who preserved them new until our day. Like the rest of the funerary equipment, they were intended for use in the other world. The lists of offerings mention antimony powder and green paint among the things sent to the *double* on festival days: the perfume ladles and boxes were as necessary in the tomb as they had been on earth.

I do not think that any survive which we can with certainty attribute to the time of the Pyramids: but the bas-reliefs of the Memphian tombs show us the joiners at work, and do not allow us to doubt that the trade in small wooden objects was very flourishing at that period. Under the great Theban Dynasties, Egypt exported them by thousands; imitated in Phœnicia, or even transported directly by the Phœnicians to the Mediterranean coasts, they transmitted the forms of Oriental art to the West. It is probable that Theban production—the only one known to us by dated monuments found in the tombs—entirely ceased, or at least became almost insignificant,

Studies in Egyptian Art

when the greatness of Thebes declined from the tenth century B.C. They were still manufactured at Memphis and in the important cities of the Delta until the Ptolemies and the Cæsars. Recent specimens are somewhat rare, and present considerable differences from those of Theban manufacture. As it was exactly this Memphian art that almost exclusively supplied the Phœnician market from the time of Sheshonq, it is vexing that examples are not more abundant : as we do not possess sufficient, we cannot accurately judge what their influence was on the arts of the Mediterranean.

The five objects I have been discussing come from the Salt collection. The Theban tombs where they were found were exploited and emptied at the beginning of the nineteenth century by collectors and dealers ; it is difficult to find any like them in Egypt now, and those that are discovered are very inferior to these in delicacy and quality.

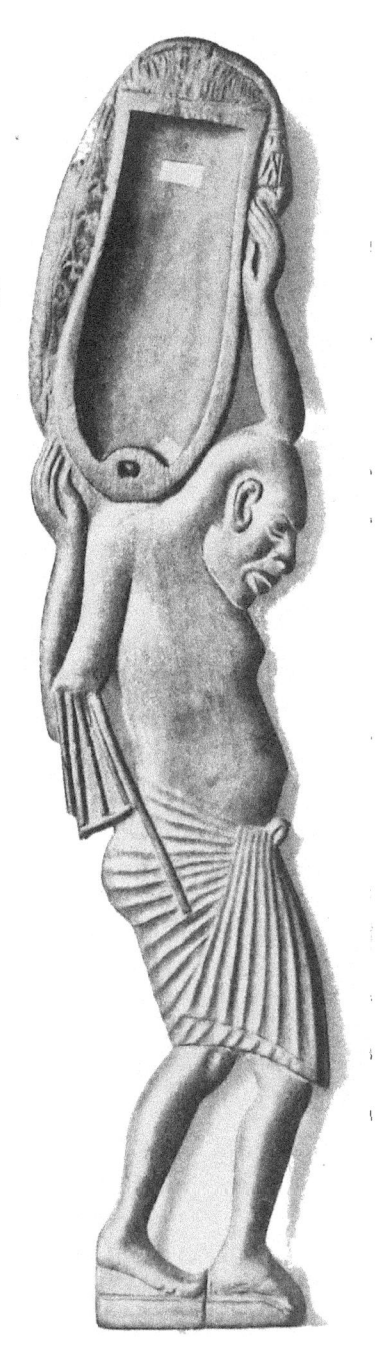

PERFUME LADLE.
The Louvre.

XXII

SOME GREEN BASALT STATUETTES OF THE SAITE PERIOD

THESE statuettes were cut in greenish basalt of fine grain, loved by the artists of the New Empire and the Saïte Period above all other stones. They formed part of the Salt collection, and are now exhibited in the Louvre.

The first represents a Pharaoh, as is proved by the serpent that rises above his forehead and the hawk's head that terminates the dagger passed through his belt. He is standing, and walking quickly, the head erect on his shoulders, and slightly bent forward in the attitude of a man who is looking attentively at the point towards which he is going; the arms are not detached from the body, and hang down along the bust and the thigh. The composition is excellent, highly finished in spite of the hardness of the material, and the detail is rendered as freely as on the colossi of the Theban Period.

The face has a particular character which struck Egyptologists long since; it is short, wide at the height of the eyes, rounded at the bottom. The eye is long, prominent, surmounted by strong curved eyebrows, marked where they join on the forehead by two deep vertical furrows. The nose is aquiline, short, thick at the

Studies in Egyptian Art

end, flanked by two nostrils the outside walls of which seem to be somewhat thin. The mouth is widely opened and protrudes; full lips, short chin receding a little under the shadow of the lips. On his return from his journey in Egypt, M. de Rougé was struck by the resemblance of this statuette, till then lying forgotten in the corner of a cupboard, with the portraits of the Shepherd Kings discovered at Sân by Mariette. Devéria cleverly reproduced it in two plates in the *Revue archéologique.** He asserted what M. de Rougé had admitted as a mere hypothesis: that it was the portrait of a Shepherd King, and that it belonged to the disturbed period which immediately preceded the XVIIIth Dynasty. I must confess that these conclusions do not appear to me to be sound. The long list of Pharaohs includes many sovereigns whose faces present characteristics very different from those usually attributed to the Egyptian race, and yet who, all the same, were Egyptians born and bred. Without entering into the discussion, I will content myself with saying that several of those who reigned at periods relatively late, Taharqa (XXVth Dynasty) or Hakori (XXIXth Dynasty) for example, bear a singular likeness to the sovereign of our statuette in the structure and expression of the face. I cannot be certain here that it is a question of one of them, but the general composition reminds me of the style of the Saïte Period more than of that of the Theban. Without asserting anything, I am inclined to believe that our Pharaoh lived in the last centuries of Egyptian independence.

The second fragment is evidently Saïte; the somewhat harsh precision of the modelling, the heaviness of the

* *Revue archéologique*, April, 1861, vol. iii., 2nd series.

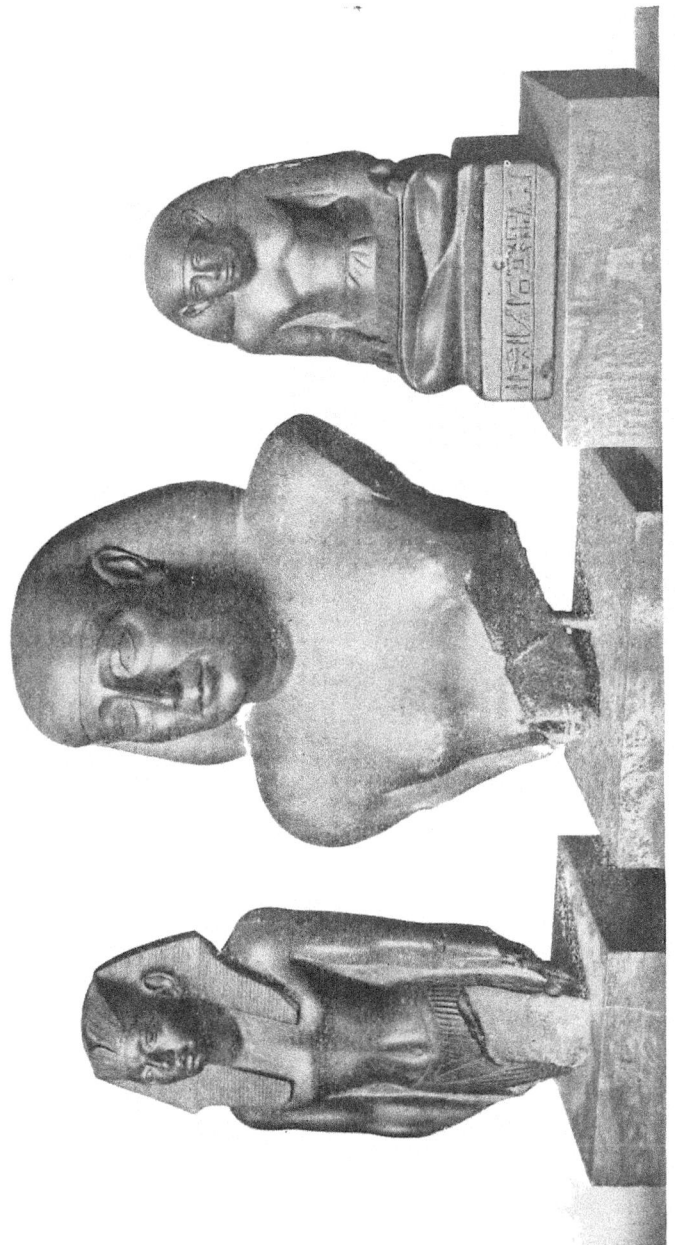

GREEN BASALT STATUETTES OF THE SAITE PERIOD.
The Louvre.

To face p. 196.

Green Basalt Statuettes

head-dress, the roundness of shoulders and chest, sufficiently prove it. It is broken too high up for us to determine if it belonged to a standing statue like the Pharaoh, or a crouching figure like the third monument. It is a perfect type of the middle-class Egyptian, developed in width rather than in height.

The shoulders are soft and flabby; the smiling insignificance of the features, the sinking down of the trunk on the hips and the head on the shoulders, are just what we should expect in one of the scribes who led sedentary lives in offices, amid piles of documents, of whom some bas-reliefs exaggerate the obesity with an evident intention of caricature. The inscription engraved on the base tells us that he was named Ai, son of Hapi, and that besides his sacerdotal functions he possessed the dignity of director of the two store-houses of the money. The Turin papyrus informs us of the nature of his office. The financial system of Egypt rested on an entirely different principle from ours: coins not being yet invented, or only lately come into use at the Saïte Period, the payment of taxes and of the officials, the transactions of the State with private individuals, or of private individuals with each other, were valued and settled in kind. Every Egyptian owed the Treasury, according to his profession and his fortune, so many fish if he was a fisherman, so many bushels of grain or head of cattle if he was an agriculturist; the whole was duly received, registered, and stored by scribes who, in their turn, put aside for the Pharaoh what would keep, and used what was perishable for the daily disbursements. Silver and gold were articles of exchange in the same way as stuffs or oxen; Pharaoh brought them back in quantities from his expeditions abroad, and received them from his subjects as the equivalent of their share of the tax. Gold

Studies in Egyptian Art

and silver circulated in powder, in sachets that contained a definite weight, in thin rings, in the form of couchant oxen, of half-oxen, of ox or gazelle heads, of jars full or empty, in curious shapes that generally were of no use in daily life, and which consequently were only, in spite of their artistic value, a sort of metallic reserve for the rich. The two store-houses or the double house of the money formed the treasury in which Pharaoh stored the quantities of gold and silver that belonged to him: taking into account the value attached to these metals, the directors of these establishments must have occupied a fairly high rank in the Egyptian hierarchy.

But for all that, we must not take the manuscript spread over Ai's knees and that he is attentively reading for an account-book, or a document relating to his business. The portion of the scroll that he holds in his right hand, placed flat on his knees, is divided into vertical columns, which, cut by horizontal lines, presents a sort of chequered surface, the squares of which are not all of the same size. Each of the larger ones contains the name of an object, and each of the smaller a number. It is the list of the gifts composing the banquet offered to the dead person on the day of burial and during the funeral ceremonies. In the tombs both of the Ancient and the New Empire it is highly developed, and comprises the most varied materials: clear or coloured waters, beers of different kinds, wines of four vintages, seven or nine of the choice pieces of the victim, cakes of all sorts, essences, cosmetics, stuffs. On the scroll of our scribe where the space was restricted the list is shortened, and we only find the actual necessities: water, beer, some meat, a little perfume. It is to that of the tombs what the usual dinner of a middle-class family is to the ceremonial banquet of

Green Basalt Statuettes

a noble; nevertheless, our scribe reads it with evident satisfaction: it is the menu of his meals for eternity, and, however scanty others may deem it, he probably considers it more pleasurable than that of his terrestrial dinners. We have here the natural development of the ideas that the Egyptians had of the other world. From the moment that the *double* was to feed materially, they sought to assure it the food of which it had need. The formulas of the stelæ which mention bread, wine, meat, deciphered by the first comer, secured the provisioning of the *double*; all that had been desired for him in reciting it would be assured him in the other world by virtue of the magic words. For lack of a passer-by to accomplish this pious duty, it occurred to them to place statues in the tomb which seemed to repeat for ever a written list held on their knees; this simulation of a perpetual reading was more than sufficient to nourish for ever the simulacrum of a man. Here, it is the defunct himself who renders himself this good office; elsewhere it is a friend, a scribe, a favourite servant.

The study of these three little monuments brings out very happily one of the qualities of Egyptian art: the skill with which the least of artists, in reproducing in a sometimes realistic manner the portrait of individuals, understood how to seize the physiognomy and bearing characteristic of their craft or of their social rank. Compare the submissive and sheepish face of the crouching scribe with the bold carriage and imperious head of the Pharaoh: the contrast is striking. With the scribe, all the muscles are relaxed; the whole body is bent, as with a man accustomed to obey and resigned to endure everything from his superiors. With the Pharaoh, the modelling is firm, the figure upright, the mien haughty; we feel that here is

Studies in Egyptian Art

a person accustomed from childhood to walk upright in the midst of bowed backs. It is unfortunate that the legend has disappeared with the lower part of the second statuette; comparing it with several other monuments in the Louvre, it reminds me of several priests of the Saïte Period. The hardness in the eye and the corners of the lips is the same, the same furrow surrounds the nostril and the mouth, the outer walls of the nose are compressed in a similar fashion; in spite of the loss of the name and titles, I am tempted to think that the individual who bears on his face in so high a degree the peculiarities of the Egyptian priest belonged to the sacerdotal caste.

XXIII

A FIND OF SAÏTE JEWELS AT SAQQARAH *

As soon as I returned to my old post, I resumed the excavations of the pyramids at the point where I had left them in 1886. I had then made a systematic search of the entrance into the funerary vaults: it was now necessary to seek out the exterior chapels, the caves, the secondary pyramids or the mastabas, which, shut in by a walled enclosure, completed the burial-place. At the end of November, 1899, I placed workmen round Ounas, and as I found it impossible to direct the operations myself with the requisite care, I entrusted the surveillance of them to M. Alexandre Barsanti, the curator-restorer of the Museum, with detailed instructions. The campaign then begun was only ended in the last days of May, 1900, and the account of it will be published elsewhere. I now wish to draw the attention of amateurs and scholars to the discovery of a mass of Saïte jewels.

The progress of the clearing away revealed the existence of a series of intact tombs at the south of the pyramid. The last of those that had been opened belonged to a very high personage named Zannehibou,

* Printed in the *Revue de l'Art ancien et moderne*, 1900, vol. viii., p. 353.

Studies in Egyptian Art

in his lifetime commandant of the king's boats. The mummy, a block of shining bitumen, was at once recognised as a very rich one. At the height of the face it had a large gold mask which fitted on the front part of the head like the *cartonnage* case usual with mummies of the second Saite Period. It had a broad necklace round its neck of beads of gold and of green felspar or of lapis lazuli mounted with gold thread, and fastened to it were numerous amulets, also of gold. Below the necklace, on the chest, an image of the goddess Nouit, in gold, spread its wings. A network of gold and felspar hung down to the hip, and from the image of the Nouit to the ankles might be read, on a long band of gold-leaf, the usual inscriptions in relief: the name of the dead man, his filiation, with short formulas of prayer. Two gold figures of Isis and Nephthys were sewn on the chest, two leaves of gold cut as sandals were fitted to the soles of the feet; a silver plaque with a line engraving of a mystic eye for the incision whence the entrails had been extracted, gold cases for the twenty fingers and toes, completed this magnificent decoration. Everything that with the lower classes of the same period would have been in cardboard, or gilded paste, or enamelled clay, was pure gold and fine stones with Zannehibou. The find, estimated by weight alone, would be valuable, but what gave it inestimable worth was the delicate and artistic workmanship of the greater number of the objects. A few of them, like the sandals and the finger-cases, are only worth the raw metal; the rest are the work of veritable artists. The inscriptions of the legs, the winged Nouit, the Isis and the Nephthys, the mask, are stamped, and although the mask and the two goddesses were miserably crushed by the lid

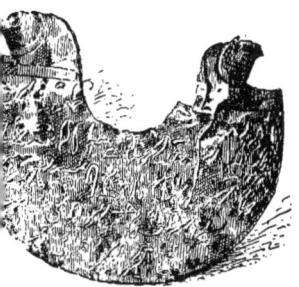

NECKLACE AMULET.

VULTURE AMULET.

GOLD PALM-TREE.

BOAT OF SOKARIS.

RAM'S HEAD.

GOLD HAWK.

HAWK WITH HUMAN HEAD.

HAWK WITH RAM'S HEAD.

VULTURE.

ISIS WITH THE CHILD.

CROUCHING NEÎTH.

A Find of Saïte Jewels at Saqqarah

when the sarcophagus was closed, the mould of hard stone which was used to fix them was so delicately cut that the best-preserved pieces, the winged Nouit, for instance, may be quoted as the highest degree of perfection that could be attained by that process. The amulet in shape of a necklace is only a leaf cut with the chisel, on which a chapter of the "Book of the Dead" is engraved with the graving needle. The vulture amulet is a small, thin plaque, on one side of which the stamped figure of a vulture with spread wings has been stuck, while on the other the chapter of the "Book of the Dead" has been engraved, as with the necklace. It is all of good workmanship, but in the amulets hanging on the real necklace of the mummy the goldsmith has surpassed himself.

They are extraordinarily small, and in order to show the detail I have had the illustrations made twice the actual size, a proceeding that weakens the contours and the modelling. To realize their beauty it is necessary to have held them in the hand. The palm-tree, which has lost some leaves, is a unique object, more curious than elegant, but the mystic boat which is beside it, unique also so far, is a prodigy of delicate chiselling. It is the boat of the god Sokaris, a boat of most archaic construction, and which was already used for the accomplishment of the sacred rites under the Thinite Dynasty. The belly is broad and round, the stern rather heavy, but the bows very light and much decorated. It rests on a sort of side-ladder of beams and ropes, which is itself built on to a sledge: it was pulled along in the public ceremonies by means of a rope put through a hole made in the curved front of the sledge. The decoration and the equipage are most

Studies in Egyptian Art

curious. On the bow is a gazelle's head with straight horns turned to the interior, and along the prow a row of divergent plates of thin metal, the use of which is not very clear: it is as if the carcase of the gazelle was opened and showed the ribs fixed on the spine. At the back, to terminate the poop, there is a ram's head with curved horns. In the middle, on an oblong rectangular pedestal, a hawk proudly perches; behind him are the four oar-rudders, two on each side; in front of him six little hawks ascend in procession, two by two, towards the gazelle's head, led by a Nile fish placed edgeways on its ventral fin. For the moment I will not attempt to explain the meaning of these emblems, but what we can never grow tired of admiring is the cleverness with which the craftsman has grouped these widely differing elements into an harmonious whole, and especially the extraordinary skill with which he worked his metal. His gazelle's head, a mere fraction of an inch in size, is of as proud a bearing as if it were of natural size: everything is exact, intelligent; the curve of the forehead, the flattening of the snout, the expression of the face, even to the natural pout of the creature. Each of the six hawks preserves its individual physiognomy, and the fish itself, reduced in size as it is, has the exact shape of the big Nile perch, and not that of any sort of fish.

Similar qualities are to be seen in the neighbouring pieces, in the ram's head, the ordinary hawk, the hawk with a human head, and that with a ram's head, and in the vulture. The seated Isis who nurses her child on her lap and the crouching Neith have their usual characteristics of resignation and gentleness, and at the same time the simplicity of line that lends so dignified an air to the smallest Egyptian figures. It has all been

MONKEYS WORSHIPPING THE EMBLEM OF OSIRIS.

VULTURE WITH EXTENDED WINGS.   HAWK WITH EXTENDED WINGS.

THE SOUL (FRONT VIEW).

THE SOUL (BACK VIEW).

A Find of Saïte Jewels at Saqqarah

chiselled out of the ingot itself, and the detail cut with so minute a point that we ask where the artisan could have obtained it.

Tiny lions addorsed or couchant, tiny mystic eyes, tiny monkeys worshipping the emblem of Osiris, tiny vultures, and tiny hawks extending their wings, each piece claims careful examination, and would by itself alone bring joy to the heart of a collector. The masterpiece of the series is, however, the *soul*, the hawk with a human head, enamelled body and wings, of which both back and front views are here reproduced. The back follows the usual manner, small rods of bent gold, curved, soldered on to a gold plaque and encrusted with thin plates of felspar to simulate feathers; but on the other side, the body, wings, and claws are modelled with the new purpose of reproducing the natural form of the bird. The little human head is a marvel of somewhat weak gracefulness: the eyes are well open, the mouth is smiling, the nostrils actually palpitate, the ear is cut out and is hollowed broad and high as is customary, and there is nothing, even to the wrinkles of the neck and the roundness of a double chin, that does not clearly stand out under the reflection of the gold. Here again, it is all chiselled by a master-hand, with a sureness I have only found in the hawk with a ram's head in the Louvre,* with which this *soul of Gizeh* may be compared.

The circumstances of the discovery would not have informed us of the date, if the style of the jewels had not done so. It is Saïte art with its lightness, suppleness, somewhat arch charm, its almost too high relief. A tendency is felt in the direction of the exaggerated roundness of the Ptolemies, and, in fact, a note furnished

* See p. 150.

Studies in Egyptian Art

by M. Chassinat permits us to fix the time at which Zannehibou lived. He belonged to the family of a certain Psammetichus, whose tomb is near his, which an inscription in the Louvre found by Mariette in the Serapeum places at the beginning of the fifth century, during the last years of the reign of Darius I. If, as is likely, he was the grandson of that Psammetichus, he died at the end of the fourth century, just when the Saïte kings were resuming their superiority over the Persians, at most, a hundred years before the Macedonian conquest. The goldsmiths who fashioned his ornaments had probably seen Greek jewels, and had perhaps already felt Hellenic influence: in that way the almost Ptolemaic characteristics of the collection are explained. We know that Saïte jewels are very rare; the Louvre alone possesses any that are out of the ordinary run: the two necklace fastenings in form of a ship bought by M. G. Bénédite a few years ago. The mummy of Zannehibou has filled up the lacuna in the Gizeh series, and thanks to it, we now know that the goldsmith's art yielded in nothing to the other arts at the time of the last Egyptian renaissance. Let us add that these jewels, although found on a mummy and made for it, are not, as is too often the case, jewels of the dead, pleasing in colour and design, but too weakly mounted to stand the wear and tear if worn by a living person. Like the jewels of Ramses II in the Louvre,* like those of Queen Ahhotpou at Gizeh, they are real jewels, identical at all points, except perhaps in the choice of subjects, with the jewels worn every day.

Such is the find that made a happy termination to our Saqqarah campaign. All the pieces were covered with bitumen, and it is no slight merit to M. Barsanti that

* See Chapter XVI., p. 145.

A Find of Saïte Jewels at Saqqarah

he should have discovered them and separated them one after the other. Several pits, equally untouched, await us at the same spot under fifteen or eighteen yards of sand, and I have a good hope that next year's excavations may have as glad surprises for us as those of this year.

XXIV

A BRONZE EGYPTIAN CAT BELONGING TO M. BARRÈRE *

THIS fine bronze cat was purchased at Cairo in 1884 by M. Barrère, then agent and consul-general of France in Egypt. It belongs to the innumerable family of cats which suddenly came forth from the ruins of Tell Bastah in 1878, and were, in a few years, scattered over the whole world. It measures 1 foot $4\frac{1}{8}$ inches in height, and if not the largest found at that time, it is at least bigger than the average. But its size is not its chief merit: the Egyptians, who were the first to tame the cat, studied it so closely that they expressed its characteristics with extraordinary excellence. M. Barrère's cat is firmly seated on her hind-quarters, looking straight in front of her, in the satisfied attitude of an animal which has done its duty and has nothing to reproach itself with. The wooden pedestal to which it was attached is wanting, but the metal tenon which fastened it is still in its place, and the body is in a perfect state of preservation. It was moulded in one piece round a core of sand that has

* Published in the *Revue de l'Art ancien et moderne*, 1902, vol. xi., p. 377.

BRONZE CAT OF THE SAÏTE PERIOD.
Barrère Collection.

A Bronze Egyptian Cat

disappeared, then touched up with the burin and the file, and then polished; it has not suffered from its long sojourn in the earth, and we can judge its qualities or its defects as clearly as if it had been made yesterday. It is a fine piece, of very sure design and careful execution. The artist was not afraid to multiply the details, and he has simplified the surfaces; but the force of the line, the robust and vigorous character of the execution, make his work a piece of the first rank. It is wonderful to note the intelligent skill with which he has expressed the characteristics and physiognomy of the race. The haunch is broad and round, the back supple, the neck slender, the head delicate, the ear straight; it is the Egyptian cat in all its elegance, as we can still see it among the fellahs, for crossing with foreign species has not altered it.

She is Bastit, a goddess of good family, the worship of whom flourished especially in the east of the delta, and she is very often drawn or named on the monuments, although they do not tell us enough of her myths or her origin. She was allied or related to the Sun, and was now said to be his sister or wife, now his daughter. She sometimes filled a beneficent and gracious rôle, protecting men against contagious diseases or evil spirits, keeping them off by the music of her sistrum: she had also her hours of treacherous perversity, during which she played with her victim as with a mouse, before finishing him off with a blow of her claws. She dwelt by preference in the city that bore her name, Poubastît, the Bubastis of classical writers. Her temple, at which Cheops and Chephrên had worked while they were building their pyramids, was rebuilt by the Pharaohs of the XXIInd Dynasty, enlarged by those of the XXVIth;

Studies in Egyptian Art

when Herodotus visited it in the middle of the fifth century B.C., he considered it one of the most remarkable he had seen in the parts of Egypt through which he had travelled. It stood in the centre of the city, at the end of the market-place. It was bordered by two canals, each 100 feet wide and shaded by trees; they flowed without joining, one on the right, the other on the left of the building, almost making it an artificial island. Travellers before entering it looked over the enclosure, even into the exterior court-yards, for Bubastis had undergone the fate of many of the large cities of Egypt; in the course of ages the ground became raised in such a way that the foundations of recent houses were on a higher level than those of the temple. A big wall, decorated with pictures like the outer wall of the temple of Edfou, enclosed the temenos. The fêtes of Bastit attracted pilgrims from all parts of Egypt, as at the present day those of Sidi Ahmed el-Bedaoui draw people to the modern fair of Tantah. The people of each village crowded into large boats to get there, men and women pell-mell, with the fixed intention of enjoying themselves on the journey, a thing they never failed to do. They accompanied the slow progress of navigation with endless songs, love songs rather than sacred hymns, and there were always to be found among them flute players and castanet players to support or keep time to the voices. Whenever they passed by a town, they approached the bank as near as they could without landing, and then, while the orchestra redoubled its noise, the passengers threw volleys of insults and coarse remarks at the women standing on the bank; they retorted, and when they had exhausted words, they pulled up their petticoats and behaved indecently by way of reply.

A Bronze Egyptian Cat

Herodotus was told that 700,000 persons, equal numbers of men and women, not reckoning little children, went thus every year to Bubastis. Entry into the temple did not calm them, far from it. They sacrificed a great number of victims with a sincere and joyous piety; then they drank deeply from morning to evening, and from evening to morning, as long as the festival lasted: more wine was consumed in a few days than in all the rest of the year put together.

The greater number of the pilgrims, before returning home, left a souvenir of their visit at the feet of Bastit. It was a votive stele with a fine inscription, and a picture showing the donor worshipping his goddess; or a statuette in blue or green pottery, or if they were wealthy, in bronze, silver, or sometimes gold: the goddess would be standing, seated, crouching with a woman's body and a cat's head, a sistrum or an ægis in her hand. During the Greek period the figures were in bronze or in painted and gilded wood surmounted by a cat's head in bronze. Many were life-size and modelled with elaborate art; they had eyes of enamel, a gilded necklace round the neck, earrings, and amulets on the forehead. It sometimes happened that when a cat he particularly venerated died in his house, the pilgrim embalmed it according to the rites: he took the mummy with him, and, arrived at Bubastis, shut it up in one of the figures he offered. These various objects, at first placed anywhere in the temple, would quickly have filled it, if some remedy had not been found. They were piled up provisionally at the end of one of the secondary chambers, then thrown outside, and there encountered diverse fortunes. I do not think I am calumniating the Egyptian priests in saying that it must have been a great grief to them to part with so

Studies in Egyptian Art

many precious gifts without trying to derive some honest profit from them. The gold and silver figures did not endure; they quickly went into the melting-pot, and few emerge from the ruins, but the bronze and copper were so abundant that there would have been little to gain in melting down the cats. So they sorted out the heap of bronzes, and while they kept some, the finest, doubtless, or those that bore inscriptions, they sold the rest to new generations of pilgrims, who, in their turn, offered them in due form. However frequently this was done, the influx was considerable, and they were forced to rid themselves quickly of the pieces that had at first been kept in reserve. They shut them up in cellars, or in pits dug expressly for them, veritable *favissæ* similar to those of classical times;* they accumulated by thousands, large and small, in wood and in bronze, some intact and fresh as when just made, others already out of shape, rotten, oxidized and of no value. The places of concealment were soon forgotten, and the stuff in them reposed there beyond the reach of men until the day when the chances of excavation brought it to light.

One of them restored M. Barrère's cat. It is not possible to determine the period at which it was buried: the persons who found it were seekers of nitreous manure, or dealers in antiquities who took good care not to divulge the circumstances and the site of their discovery. But judging from the roundness of certain forms and the aspect of the bronze, we recognize the style of the second Saïte Period, and the piece is to be attributed either to the Nectanebos, or the first Ptolemies, in a general way to the fourth century B.C. or the beginning of the third century B.C. It was the time when the worship of Bastit

* See Chapter X.

A Bronze Egyptian Cat

and her subordinate forms, Pakhît, Maît, was most popular, the period when, near Speos-Artemidos, the most extensive cemetery of cats in Egypt was established. The execution is pure Egyptian, and in no way betrays any Greek influence.

XXV

A FIND OF CATS IN EGYPT[*]

It was announced in the English newspapers, and the French followed suit, that a ship had recently reached London and disembarked 180,000 mummies of Egyptian cats. For a long time manufacturers of different nationalities have been accustomed to seek out the burying grounds of animals throughout Egypt, and to export the bones to Europe, where they are used as manure. A few years ago a necropolis full of monkeys was sent to Germany to manure beet-root fields. It seems that the cats of this year were discovered near Beni-Hassan; they were piled up at hazard in a sort of cavern, into which a fellah in search of antiquities was the first to penetrate. In fact, at some distance to the south of the hypogeums of Beni-Hassan, in the place called by geographers Speos-Artemidos, is a chapel hollowed out in the rock, and consecrated by the kings of the XVIIIth and XIXth Dynasties to a local goddess, a woman's body with a cat's or lion's head, called Pakhît. The depôt recently exploited was found there, and the cats which reposed in it must have lived in the vicinity, under the protection of their cousin, the goddess. Cemeteries of the same kind existed wherever a divinity of a feline type was worshipped,

[*] Published in *La Nature*, 1890, vol. xxxv., pp. 273–4.

BRONZE CAT.
The Louvre

A Find of Cats in Egypt

lion, tiger, or cat. The most celebrated was at Bubastis, in the delta, where the seekers of antiquities cleared away the rubbish about thirty-seven years ago.* The mummies of cats were buried there in *favissæ*, deep pits, some merely wrapped in swathings, others enclosed in little coffins reproducing the image of the animal. Some of these coffins are entirely of wood covered with white stucco, gilded, painted in bright colours; some are in bronze, others have the body in wood and the head in bronze, with gold rings in their ears and encrustations of gold on the forehead and in the eyes. Statuettes of cats of different sizes, portraits of the goddess Bastit with a cat's head, or of the god Nofirtoumou, are mingled with the mummies. Thence come the thousands of bronze cats, big and little, with which all the antiquaries of Europe and Cairo were so abundantly provided from 1876 to 1888. The important cat illustrated here, and who lives now in one of the glass cases in the " Salle divine " of the Louvre, is a perfect type of the species, long, slender in the back, broad in the hind-quarters, with a delicate, well-set head, rings in the ears, a necklace round the neck, and a little scarab on the top of the head; the artist who modelled it has rendered excellently and truthfully the supple bearing and the bold physiognomy of his original.

The cats represented on the monuments, or the mummies of which are found in Egypt, were not of the same race as our domestic cat. Scholars have studied them and are unanimous—Virchow, too, recently—in recognizing them as the *Felis maniculata* and the *Felis chaus*. Egypt had tamed a few individual ones, but had not domesticated the whole species. They are sometimes to be seen on the bas-reliefs solemnly seated

* See pp. 212–213.

Studies in Egyptian Art

near their masters. It is commonly asserted that they were used for hunting birds in the marshes, and Wilkinson quotes in support a fairly large number of mural paintings where they stalk through the reeds, routing out little birds. I confess that this interpretation does not seem to me to be correct. Where others claim to recognize animals ready for the chase and acting on behalf of man, I only see animals, tame or not, on marauding bent and scouring the bushes for their own purposes; just as our domesticated cat chases the sparrows in our gardens and destroys the nests in our parks without any advantage to his master. Egyptian artists, very acute observers of what was going on around them, reproduced their cats' expeditions, as they noted other picturesque details of the life of nature.

If we examined the 180,000 cats—neither more nor less—we should probably come upon a fairly large proportion of ichneumons. In Egypt the ichneumon and the cat were always associated; wherever there are mummies of cats it may be safely assumed that mummies of ichneumons are not far off. Cats or ichneumons, I hope the whole of them will not be used to manure the ground, but that some fine specimens may be chosen for the museums of antiquities and of natural history: in sparing a few hundreds, agriculture will not lose much, and science will gain considerably. The origin of our tom-cat has long been under discussion; some refer it to Egypt, others to Europe. It would be a pity not to profit by such an invasion of Egyptian cats, and to try to obtain a definite solution of the question.

INDEX

A

Abousîr-el-Malak, excavations of, 29
Abydos, 30, 31, 37; Memnonium of, 95, 134; ruins of, 94
Adoni (Adonaï), 122
Ahhotpou I, 145, 146, 158
Ahhotpou, Queen, 152, 158, 206
Ahmôsis I, 138
Aî, 138; portrait of, 98
Aî, son of Hapi, 197, 198
Alexandria, bas-reliefs of, 33
Amenemhaît III, 26, 32; sphinx of, 22, 23; statue of, 22, 28, 37
Amenertaîous, 103
Amenhotpou, 138
Amenmeses, 138
Amenôphis II, 122
Amenôphis III, 122, 124, 174
Amenôphis IV, 120, 122, 123, 124, 125, 131
Amenôphis, statue of, 64
Amenôthes I, 91
Amenôthes II, 109, 112, 113, 117, 118, 134
Amenôthes IV, 31
Amenôthes, statue of, 22, 28
Amon, 81, 101, 102, 104, 121, 122, 124, 125, 135, 183, 184, 185; priests of, 92; temple of, 90, 97, 137

Amon of Harmhabi, 98
Amonrâ, 107, 123
Amonrâ, ark of, 136
Anderson, 142
Ankhari, *the lady*, 175
Ankhasnofiriabrê en Hathor, 103
Ankhnas, 103
Antonf kings, the, 153
Anubis, temple of, 53
Apis, 146, 149; tomb of, 79, 145
Apouî, tomb of, 21
Apries, 143
Armaïs, 139
Asia Minor, 169, 191
Assiout, 31
Assyria, 169
Ati, 56, 58, 59
Aton (Amon), 121, 122, 123, 124, 125
Atonian Dynasty, fall of the, 31

B

Bagnold, Major Arthur, 142, 143
Baraize, M., 108
Barrère, M., 208, 212
Barsanti, M. Alexandre, 201, 206
Bastit, the goddess, 184, 209, 212, 213, 215; her festival at Bubastis, 210, 211
Baÿ, Dr., 133

Index

Bedrechein, 141
Bénédite, M., 206
Beni-Hassan, 30, 31, 87, 214
Berbers, the, 129
Bercheh, 31
Berlin Museum, 152; *Scribe* of the, 20, 21
Bibân-el-Molouk, 111
Bissing, F. W. von, 17, 18, 20, 21, 22, 23, 24, 25, 26, 27, 34, 35
Bocchoris, 33
"Book of the Dead," 113, 114, 203
Borchardt, 24, 25
Boulaq Museum, 63, 70, 71, 81, 85, 86, 135, 137, 138, 145, 146
British Museum, 153
Bruckmann, 17, 23
Bubastis, 124, 154, 157, 161, 190, 210, 211, 215

C

Cairo, 39, 108, 154, 179, 208, 215
Cairo Museum, the, 21, 22, 29, 32, 33, 39, 44, 46, 47, 93, 96, 98, 108, 114, 115, 116, 128, 129, 131, 134, 157; *Scribe* of the, 20
Carter, 92
Caviglia, 141
Chaldæa, 169, 171
Champollion, 121, 172, 186
Chassinat, M., 206
Cheîkh-Abd-el-Gournah, 115, 178, 179
Cheîkh el-Beled, statue of the, 21, 46, 48, 88

Cheîkh-Said, 31
Cheops, 30, 209; statuette of, 37, 38
Chephrên, 30, 44, 46, 47, 48, 137, 209; statuette of, 37, 38
Chephrên, statues of the, 21, 24, 37
Coptos, 22
Cow, the, of Deîr-el-Bahari, 18, 106, 117
Crete, 169
Crouching Scribe, the, 18, 48, 49, 60, 61, 63, 64, 65, 84, 88

D

Dahchour, 145, 150, 152, 158
Darius, 140, 206
Davis, Theodore, 126
Decauville, 90
Denderah, 31, 123
Deîr-el-Bahari, 92, 108, 110, 115; *favissa* of, 98; porticoes of, 95
Dévéria, 196
Dog, nome of the, 41
Double, the, 51, 52, 53, 54, 111, 115, 143, 193, 198

E

Ebers, 17
Edfou, temple of, 210
Edgar, Mr., 154, 155
Egypt, financial system of ancient, 197, 198
Egyptian cats, 208, 209, 214, 215, 216
Egyptian jewellery, 145-153; 201-207

Index

Egyptian Scribes, 61, 62, 63, 67, 68, 69, 74, 75, 76, 77, 199, 200
Egyptian statuary, 17–35
El-Amarna, bas-reliefs of, 131; necropolis of, 31, 125, 133; sculptors of, 130; statues of, 100
El-Tell, tombs of, 31
Es-Sayed Eïd, 155
Ethiopia, 95, 102, 124, 139
Ethiopian pyramids, the, 153
Euphrates, 170
Europe, 215, 216

F

Fayoum, the, 26, 29, 94, 137
Ferlini, 153

G

Garwood, 142
Gebeleîn, 22, 179, 214
Germany, 214
Gizeh, 39, 95
Gizeh Museum, 21, 24, 66, 68, 70, 152, 206
Gizeh, necropolis of, 21, 29
Gold and silver vases and cups, 160–8
Golenischeff, 32
Gournah, 138
Gournah, temple of, 95, 134
Grébaut, 37
Greece, 119

H

Hachopsouïtou, Queen, 97, 111, 112, 119
Hakori, 196
Hapi-T'aufi, Prince, 53

Harmais, statues of the, 22
Harmhâbi, 100, 130, 133, 135, 138, 139
Hathor, the goddess, 41, 42, 109, 110, 111, 112, 114, 115, 117, 118, 187
Heliopolis, 123
Hellenes, the, 33
Heracleopolis, 30, 94
Hermopolis, 28, 31, 105
Herodotus, 32, 124, 140, 210, 211
Hor, the scribe, 84
Horus, 188
Horus Qa-âou, stele of the, 19
Hrihor, 124
Hyksôs king, portrait of a, 22

I

Icelanders and ghosts, 176
Iouaa, 122
Isis, 97, 116, 147, 148, 202, 204
Isis, statue of, 96

K

Karnak, 31, 37, 105, 138, 139; *favissa* of, 22, 26, 90, 94, 95, 96; modern village of, 90; temple of, 135
Khâbokhni, 188
Khâmoîsît, high priest of Phtah, 145, 146
Khâsakhmouï, the Pharaoh, 19, 20
Khitas, the, 151
Khnoum, 135
Khnoumhotpou, the dwarf, 85, 86, 87, 88, 89

Index

Khonsou, 98, 99
Khounaton, 125, 138
Khouniatonou, 31, 100, 126, 130, 133
Kings, Valley of the, 126
King-Serpent, stele of the, 19
Knom, 56, 58

L

Leghorn, 172
Legrain, M., 22, 26, 91, 94, 95, 96, 98, 100, 105
Lepsius, 57
Leyden, 20
Leyden Museum, 153, 175
Leyden papyrus, the, 177
Libyan Desert, the, 112
Libyan Mountains, the, 113
Longpérier, M. de, 49
Louis XIV, peruke of time of, 180
Louvre, the, 18, 21, 22, 49, 54, 55, 58, 60, 64, 67, 68, 70, 79, 80, 84, 125, 130, 134, 136, 145, 146, 152, 153, 172, 178, 183, 185, 186, 195, 200, 205, 206, 215
Louxor, 31, 107

M

Macedonians, the, 102
Madagascar, queens of, 104
Maît, 213
Mankahorou, statuette of, 37
Mantimehê, 103, 104
Mariette, 22, 24, 32, 38, 55, 60, 62, 66, 79, 94, 98, 100, 103, 116, 121, 136, 139, 145, 150, 151, 196, 206

Matonou (Amten), statue of, at Berlin, 29
Medinet Habou, 128
Mediterranean, the, 171, 194
Meîdoum, 46, 48, 62, 63; excavations of, 29, 30
Memphian Empire, the, 20
Memphis, 25, 28, 29, 30, 31, 32, 37, 55, 72, 78, 79, 88, 123, 137, 140
Menephtah, 136, 138
Menna, 182
Menzaleh, Lake, 32
Minieh, prince of, 85, 87
Minou, the god, 22
Mît-Fares, 22
Mît-Rahineh, 24, 37, 39
Mohammed-Ali, 142
Mohammed Effendi Chaban, 154
Mond, Mr., 178
Montouhotpou, 111
Montouhotpou, statue of, 26
Montouhotpou I, temple of, 22, 106
Montouhotpou III, statue of, 22
Montouhotpou V, tomb of, 92
Monuments de l'Art Antique, 34
Morgan, M. de, 66, 73, 145
Moursi Hassaneîn, 155
Munich, 20, 21
Musée Egyptien, the, 26, 34
Mycerinus, statues of, 36, 37, 38, 39, 41, 43, 44, 46, 47, 48

N

Nafêrourîya, 97
Naî, the lady, 173, 174, 177, 186

Index

Naousirrîya, statuette of, 37
Napata, 31
Naples Museum, the, 20
Nâr-mer, *palette* of, 19
Nasi, statue of, 21
Naville, 92, 106, 107, 111, 118
Nectanebo I, 116
Nectanebo II, 33
Neîth, 204; temple of, 167, 169
Nephthys, 147, 148, 202
Nile, the, 27, 112, 170; valley of the, 28
Nofirtoumou, the god, 215
Nofrihotpou, funeral of, 88
Nofrît, statue of, 22
Nonît, the goddess, 202
Nsiphtah, 103
Nubia, 31

O

Omm-el-Gaâb, tombs of, 29
Osiris, 116, 123, 147, 148, 205
Osorkon II, statuette of, 103
Ostraca, 98
Ounas, 201
Ousimares (Osymandyas), 158
Ousirmâri, 149
Oxyrrhinchus, 41

P

Pakhît, 213, 214
Pehournowri, statuette of, 79, 84
Perfume ladles described, 190-3
Persian Conquest, the, 91
Persians, the, 104
Petesomtous, 116

Petrie, Flinders, 26, 47, 129, 131
Phœnicia, 193
Phœnicians, the, 171
Phtah, 87, 95, 141, 145, 173; temple of, 37, 140
Phtah-Maî, 173, 174
Pioupi, bronze statue of, 21
Poubastît (Bubastis), 209
Psammetichus, 116, 117, 206
Psammetichus I, 33, 103
Psarou, 146, 147
Pyramids, plain of the, 29

Q

Qodshou, battle of, 151

R

Râ, the solar god, 123, 124
Rahotpou, the scribe, 84; tomb of, 62
Ramessides, the, 91, 103, 124
Ramke, the scribe, 84
Ramses, 130; statues of the, 22
Ramses I, 138
Ramses II, 30, 136, 137, 138, 140, 141, 142, 144, 145, 148, 151, 158, 159, 160, 170, 206; statues of, 26, 101, 135
Ramses III, 102
Ramses VI, 101, 102
Ramses-Nakhouîti, 101
Rânofir, 44, 46, 88; statue of, 70, 71, 72, 77, 78
Readers, statue of the, at Cairo, 21
Reisner, 39, 44

Index

Rome, 119
Rougé, M. de, 196
Roxelane, 127

S

Sabou, tomb of, 66
Saïd, the, 31, 113
St. Sebastian, paintings of, 83, 84
Saïs, 105
Saïte jewels, 201
Saladin, 39
Salt Collection, the, 120, 194
Sân, 196
Sânakht, 138
Sanmaout, statue of, 96, 97
Sanouosrît I, statue of, 22, 46; bas-relief of, 22, 37; (Ousirtasen), 94, 95
Sanouosrît III, 94; statue of, 46
Sapouî (Sepa), statue of, in the Louvre, 21, 29, 64
Saqqarah, necropolises of, 21, 29, 49, 55, 63, 66, 76, 85, 88, 95; village of, 72
Sculpture in wood, 172-4, 183-9
Scythians, the, 140
Serapeum, the, 55, 60, 64, 79, 145, 146, 148, 150, 153, 206
Serdâb, the, 51, 60, 62
"Service des Antiquités," the, 143, 155, 178
Sesostris, 140
Setinakht, 138
Setouî I, 30, 37, 95, 121, 130, 138; hypogeum of, 134; statue of, 135
Setouî II, 138, 160

Shepherd Kings, the, 22, 32; portraits of, 196
Sheshonq, 194
Sidi Ahmed el-Bedaouî, 210
Simon, Herr, of Berlin, 129
Sinai, 129
Siout, 54
Siphtah, 160
Siphtah Menephtah, 138
Sistrum, nome of the, 41
Skhemka, the scribe, 55, 56, 58, 59, 60, 64, 65, 84
Sokaris, boat of the god, 203
Sovkemsaouf, 22
Sovkhotpou, the king, 22, 84
Speos-Artemidos, cemetery of cats at, 213, 214
Sphinxes, the so-called Hyksôs, 28, 32
Stephenson, General, 142
Sycomore, Canton of the, 41
Syria, 95, 124, 139, 164, 171

T

Taharkou, 103
Taharqa, 196
Taïa, 98, 99, 121, 122, 134
Tamaî, singing-girl of Neîth, 167, 169
Tanis, 32, 102, 105, 137; sphinxes of, 28
Tantah, fair of, 210
Taouasrît, 170
Tboubouî, 184
Tell Bastah, ruins of, 208
Tell-el-Khanzir, 142
Thebaïd, the, 102

222

Index

Theban Empire, the, 21, 22, 28, 32
Thebes, 28, 30, 31, 88, 92, 93, 95, 105, 120, 123, 124, 125, 128, 131, 137, 145, 181, 183, 187
Thebes, government of, 103, 104
Thinis, 30
Thinis-Abydos, 29
Thinites, the, 20, 29
Thot, city of, 31
Thoutmôsis, 138
Thoutmôsis, statue of, 22
Thoutmôsis III, 91, 94, 96, 97, 98, 107, 109, 112, 121, 134
Thoutmôsis IV, 124
Tî, 88; statue of, 70
Tîyi, 126, 127, 128, 129
Tîyi, wife of Amenôthes III, 100
Touaa, 122
Touî, the lady, 178, 183, 184, 185, 186, 189
Toumoumtaouneb, the royal cup-bearer, 164
Tourah, limestone of, 49, 179

Toutânkhamânou, 133, 134, 138
Toutânoukhamanou, 98, 99, 100
Turin Museum, 64, 183, 186, 189
Turin papyrus, the, 197

U

Upper Egypt, 41

V

Vassalli, 47
Vienna Museum, 22
Virchow, 215

W

Wiedemann, 26
Wilkinson, 216

Z

Zagazig, 154, 155, 156, 165, 171
Zannehibou, 201, 202, 206

www.ingramcontent.com/pod-product-compliance
Lightning Source LLC
Chambersburg PA
CBHW050901240426
43668CB00028B/2425